PRAISE FOR GALATIANS: *A*

MW00534006

Combining the knowledg sensitively of a parish minister, and the creativity of a seasoned writer, Bruce Epperly roots his study of Paul's letter to the Galatians in its historical and literary context while bringing it right to the time of today's readers. His ability to bring these two worlds together by making us Galatians for our own time opens afresh for us this revolutionary and liberating epistle, which argues that the gospel of God's revelation in Jesus is open to all. Indeed, as Epperly points out, "Paul's open-spirited and – dare I say – radical and progressive message enabled the Christian movement to become global in scope." While maintaining his focus on Galatians, Epperly also works in passages from some of Paul's other letters, showing readers Paul's concern for maintaining unity and diversity across Christianity in the first century as the gospel spread to diverse communities. Those same concerns appeal to Christians in the 21st century; perhaps even more so. Epperly passionately uses Paul's words to remind Christians today that we are free in Christ, but that such "freedom finds its fullest expression in loving relationships that take into consideration the needs of others." I highly recommend *Galatians: A Participatory Guide* to anyone, but especially to Christian communities who are seeking not only to read Galatians together, but who desire to be transformed by its liberating power.

C. Drew Smith, Ph.D.
Author of *Reframing a Relevant Faith*,
Director of the Center for International Programs
Henderson State University, AR

Bruce Epperly's work is one of a pastoral genius. He doesn't sacrifice the academic, but finds a way to make what the academy has been doing for the past 50 years actually usable. Rather than a dry rehashing of either Reformation-era theology or a classroom lecture, Epperly treats Galatians as if it was a spiritual discipline, allowing us the chance to read it, pray it, and live it.

Joel Watts, *Unsettled Christianity*.com
and author of *From Fear to Faith*, Charleston, WV

Bruce Epperly's work on Galatians is a welcome breath of fresh air for local congregations who want to engage the Scriptures with both head and heart. Weaving together multiple forms of critical biblical study in an accessible narrative, Epperly provides a thought-provoking and spirit-enlivening window into this Pauline letter, offering insight into the biblical world at the same time as inviting relevant conversation about how this letter speaks to communities in this age.

As a pastor in a large urban church whose congregants run the gamut from life-long Christians to those new to any spiritual journey, this study guide uniquely provides material that can feed and stimulate participants from a wide range of backgrounds, experience and knowledge. For those who are looking for individual or small group study material that not only encourages but insists on questioning and wrestling with the biblical text in the midst of people's own contexts, this study will not disappoint.

Epperly's work offers not only intellectual engagement with the text but also provides tools for multiple forms of prayerful encounter. Drawing on ancient and new traditions, he encourages students of Scripture to allow the Spirit to speak to them as they listen for what the text says to their own lives. Rarely do biblical study guides provide quality critical analysis along with multiple models of spiritual discernment. Providing both offers individuals and group leaders a creative space in which to shape their study of Galatians.

This guide is one that will allow those who have been turned off by biblical studies that ignore both current critical thinking on scripture and the world around them to engage the texts again with renewed hope for finding a word of truth for their lives.

Rev. Sandra K. Olewine, Pastor
First United Methodist Church, Pasadena, CA

GALATIANS:

A PARTICIPATORY STUDY GUIDE

BRUCE G. EPPERLY

Energion Publications
Gonzalez, FL
2015

Copyright © 2015, Bruce G. Epperly

Unless otherwise indicated, all Scripture quotations are from the New Revised Standard Version Bible, copyright © 1989 by the Division of Christian Education of the National Council of the Churches of Christ in the U. S. A. Used by permission. All rights reserved.

ISBN10: 1-63199-169-8
ISBN13: 978-1-63199-169-1
Library of Congress Control Number: 2015945369

Energion Publications
P. O. Box 841
Gonzalez, FL 32560

energion.com
pubs@energion.com

DEDICATION

To the faithful community of South Congregational Church, Centerville, Massachusetts,and my wife Kate whose love inspires my creativity and commitment.

THE PARTICIPATORY STUDY SERIES

The Participatory Study Series from Energion Publications is designed to invite Bible students to become a part of the community of faith that produced the texts we now have as Scripture by studying them empathetically and with an aim to learn and grow spiritually.

The section on using this book, titled "Becoming Galation: Spiritual Practices for Reading Galatians" in this volume, and the appendices are designed for the series and adapted to the particular study guide. Each author is free to emphasize different resources in the study, and individual students, group leaders, and teachers are encouraged to enhance their study through the use of additional resources.

It is our prayer at Energion Publications that each study guide will lead you deeper into Scripture and more importantly closer to the One who inspired it.

— Henry Neufeld, General Editor

TABLE OF CONTENTS

PREFACE

A MOVEMENT IN THE MAKING

German political leader Otto von Bismarck (1815-1898) once asserted that the making of laws is like making sausage. Sausage making is messy business and the ingredients might surprise you! Accordingly, it is better not to see sausages being made if you plan on eating them later! This same judgment may apply to the formation of the early Christian movement. Today's apparent stability of denominational structures, creeds and doctrines, ordained ministry, and the existence of scriptures that are particularly Christian, the New Testament, give us the illusion that the Christian faith was fully formed from the very beginning just the way Jesus intended it and that there was a clear and unambiguous understanding of Jesus' message and the meaning of the cross. In truth, during the first decades following Pentecost, the earliest followers of Jesus made it up as they went along, and often had very different understandings of Jesus' message and impact on humankind. Many received their instruction through what they perceived to be direct encounters with the Holy Spirit, while others had heard Jesus' message and experienced his healing miracles first-hand. Still others experienced Jesus through the radical hospitality and countercultural spirit of the first Christian communities. Some affirmed the significance of the Jewish tradition in the formation of Christians; others believed that Jesus' message could be completely separated from his Jewish roots to the point of eliminating the Old Testament entirely from Christian theology.[1]

---

1 For a picture of the early church see Bruce Epperly, *Transforming Acts* (Gonzalez, FL: Energion Publications, 2013).

In the first few decades of the Jesus movement, new believers, like Jesus' first male and female followers, experienced the gifts of the Spirit, manifest in ecstatic experiences, transformed lives, and healing touch. But they had no scriptures of their own, nor did they have creedal statements or stable institutional structures. They had key leaders, such as James the brother of Jesus, Peter, and later the Apostle Paul, but no universal and fully agreed upon beliefs or rituals. They had the Jewish scriptures, traditions, and rituals, and the stories of Jesus, passed on from one follower to another and recited within the early Christian communities. But the Jewish rituals initially meant little or nothing to non-Jewish followers of Jesus.

The emerging faith was open-spirited and unformed. What it might become in the decades ahead was anyone's guess. In fact, there were many varieties of Christian faith emerging in the first decades of the Jesus movement. Later, some were declared heresies, for example, certain world and body denying philosophies and spiritual practices, often labeled as Gnostic, as well as unbridled charismatic movements led by those who saw themselves as direct conduits of the Holy Spirit's wisdom, the Montanists. It is clear that there was diversity of theology, practice, and experience in the early Jesus movement, some of which, in the course of centuries, gave birth to the diverse theological and worship styles of our time.

In this dynamic and open-ended context, Paul's Letter to the Galatians emerged and eventually gained the status of scripture. The Jewish sect, inspired by the Galilean healer and teacher, was going global and Paul was, according to Acts of the Apostles and his own affirmation, its leading messenger. In the course of his ministry, Paul founded churches throughout the Mediterranean world. Paul's authority and apostleship were grounded in an audacious claim. Despite the fact he had persecuted the first followers of Jesus, he claimed that God had chosen him for a particular spiritual task. Paul had encountered the Risen One on the road to Damascus and he believed that this encounter gave him the same authority as Jesus' first disciples. Paul's mystical experience of the

Risen One came with the call to mission. The Risen Christ gave Paul the vocation of sharing God's good news with the Gentiles, the ethnic and religious outsiders he once viewed as spiritual inferiors.

The region of Galatia was at the heart of Paul's mandate to reach out to the Gentiles. Journeying from his home base, as some scholars believe, Antioch in today's Syria, Paul shared the good news in what is today central Turkey. He helped shape and may have planted small Christian communities in towns such as Derbe, Lystra, Iconium, and Antioch of Pisidia. Paul's straightforward message of spiritual liberation touched the hearts of many Gentiles. The good news of Christ's death and resurrection and the opportunity for new life in Christ inspired mystical and charismatic experiences and no doubt "signs and wonders" in the communities Paul founded. Some new members of the Jesus movement cried out "Abba, Father," in response to the liberating news of God's grace in Jesus Christ. They were, as Paul writes in the Letter to the Galatians, spiritually free and untrammeled by ritual and doctrine, including those of Jesus' own religious tradition. They experienced themselves as new creations, freed from sin and guilt, as the spirit of Christ transformed them, body, mind, and spirit.

But spiritual honeymoons, like relational honeymoons, don't usually last forever. As in the case with couples who fall in love, the initial excitement and belief that "love conquers all" often gives way to old habits and patterns of behavior. Paul heard stories of churches in trouble and reverting to past behaviors and belief systems. Rumors surfaced that his word of grace was being compromised by those who taught a return to Jewish dietary and spiritual practices, most particularly ethnically-separate table fellowship and male circumcision. Paul's tone is angry and urgent. The fate of the Galatian churches and his mission to the Gentiles was at stake.

Galatians is no armchair theology, but a passionate argument for the grace of God, the unity of the church, and the equality of all Christians, despite differences in ethnicity, social standing, economics, and sexuality. In the providence of God, Paul's letter was preserved and his faith vindicated. As New Testament scholar N.T. Wright asserts, Paul's passionate Galatian letter gave birth to Christian theology. As I told my Galatians Bible study participants at South Congregational Church, we are here as Gentiles because of Paul's message to the Galatians. Apart from Paul's clarion call to Christian freedom, the Jesus movement might have remained a Jewish sect, defined by its adherence to the Jewish law, dietary habits, and practice of circumcision. Paul's open-spirited and – dare I say – radical and progressive message enabled the Christian movement to become global in scope. The global reach of the gospel depended on its message becoming accessible to people in every time and place, beginning with the Gentile communities of the Roman Empire.

Paul's passion is to share the good news without hindrance of culture or ritual. Accordingly, putting burdens on Gentile believers stands in the way of spreading Christ's message of salvation. As N.T. Wright asserts, "it is absolutely imperative that all those 'in the Messiah' belong to the same table. Separation is not an option."[2]

Galatians has been described as one of the greatest pieces of religious literature. Paul's passionate message shaped the Christian vision of grace, faith, biblical interpretation and unity. These are still issues for us as we make it up as we go along in the context of our pluralistic and postmodern spiritual landscape.

From the perspective of biblical scholarship, the Letter to the Galatians "presented a glimpse of the controversy that surrounded the expansion of the Christian movement into the Gentile communities of the Mediterranean world."[3] Galatians was one of the formative texts of the sixteenth Protestant Reformation. Although Martin Luther may have seen – and thus to some extent distorted – Paul's message in light of his own experience of guilt and grace and subsequent conflict with the Roman church, whom he identified

---

2 N.T. Wright, *Paul and the Faithfulness of God,* volume 1, (Minneapolis: Fortress Press, 2013), 359.

3 Richard Hays, *Galatians. The New Interpreter's Bible. XI. (Nashville: Abingdon, 2000),* 183.

with Jewish legalism, its message has nevertheless transformed lives and provided a normative vision of conversion experiences. Perhaps, beyond Paul's original intent, Galatians, along with the Letter to the Romans, has shaped the contours of grace and provided a template for understanding God's ability to transform persecutors into proclaimers and sinners into saints.

Galatians is a contemporary book. It asks us to consider the boundaries of Christian faith. It invites us to discern what is theologically and behaviorally essential to Christianity. Galatians has been an inspiration in the fight for equality in the church and the world for women, minorities, and most recently gay and lesbian persons. Galatians takes Jesus' vision of radical hospitality and applies it to the real and imperfect churches where we worship. Accordingly, its message encourages personal spiritual freedom and the liberation of institutional structures.

Reflecting what John Dominic Crossan and Marcus Borg describe as the "radical Paul," Galatians has been described as the magna carta of Christian freedom through its portrayal of open ended faith without fences or boundaries. Today's readers of the letter to Galatians are challenged to affirm both diversity and unity in Christian experience and, in the process, extend our freedom in the body of Christ to the whole world.

As you begin your Galatians journey, remember Paul's message of graceful transformation: in light of God's suffering love on Calvary, what matters above all else is God's new creation in your life and in your congregation. Let Paul's passionate faith inspire you to embrace God's wondrous diversity, whether in theological and liturgical differences in your congregation or Bible study group, and the various expressions of divine creativity in culture, ethnicity, and sexuality. Let the call to Christian unity guide your group conversations, inspiring you to listen and respond in ways that build bridges rather than walls.

A Word of Thanks and a Word on Perspective

Every commentator has a perspective, which shapes her or his understanding of scripture, and I am no exception. Raised in the evangelical wing of the American Baptist Churches, I grew up with revival preachers and altar calls as well as my Baptist minister father's more low key approach to the gospel. The message I often heard was that we were sinners saved by grace, and transformed by Jesus' sacrificial death on the cross on Calvary's hill. It was that message that inspired me to "come forward" with tears in my eyes at nine years of age, dying to sin and accepting Jesus as my personal savior. As a teen, I found this small town evangelical faith too spiritually confining and too certain of itself and became as student and practitioner of Buddhism and Hinduism as well as North American Transcendentalism. Eventually, my journey led me back to grace, that is, Grace Baptist Church, in San Jose, California, where a long-haired college student was welcomed with all his questions and doubts. It was at Grace Baptist that I began to formulate my own theology, a creative synthesis of evangelical experience, mystical experiences, spiritual practices, and progressive process theology.

I am still a child of grace. I come at scripture as a living word, whose purpose is to liberate and transform. Scripture is the beginning and not the end of our spiritual journeys. Scripture invites us to be part of God's holy adventure in our time and place, taking our place as the receivers and creators of the Christian message in our time. Like the first followers of the Risen Jesus, we create the meaning of grace in light of the concrete challenges and stresses of our time. In the spirit of their Hebraic parents, the New Testament authors experienced God's presence in life-changing ways and shared that experience from their own particular perspective on Jesus' message and work of salvation, and so do we.

Paul's words to the Galatian communities are passionate, life-transforming, and faith-defining but they are not inerrant. No doubt Peter, whom Paul criticized, felt just as inspired by God as did Paul. James, the brother of Jesus and leader of the Jerusalem church, may have found both Peter and Paul too open-minded and liberal in their openness to Gentile culture and experience.

Paul's passion and imaginative use of scripture invites us to be innovative in our scripture reading. A living word requires us to go beyond the words of scripture to discover God's Spirit speaking in what is said and unsaid. In my own encounter with scripture, I read scripture as a source book of spiritual affirmations and pathways to discipleship. Read affirmatively, Galatians and its New Testament companions are good news revealing God's loving vision to people in the first century as well as our own. They liberate us from the constraints of an unhealthy and irrelevant past and open us to God's new creation.

I believe that God's revelation is ongoing, global, and constantly new. As the United Church of Christ motto proclaims, "God is still speaking" and we need to listen to God's many voices in scripture, science, literature, culture, and religious experience. Paul believed that his word was authoritative, but not final. Paul assumed our understanding of God was incomplete. "We see in a mirror dimly" and "know only in part" and will more fully understand when we come face to face with God (1 Corinthians 13:9-12). In that spirit, my own reading is progressive, open-spirited, evangelical, and mystical in orientation. I recognize that my approach is one of many possible interpretations of Paul's passionate letter. Others will discover hints of the doctrine of substitutionary atonement, salvation by Christ alone, Christian superiority, or Pauline paternalism and sexism as they turn the pages of Galatians. Still others will find in Galatians a word of welcome, liberating us to be ourselves honestly and authentically in relationship to God and one another.

I believe that we can, like Paul, encounter God and be forever changed. That's ultimately why I am writing this commentary; so that all who read this may experience transformation through encountering the living Christ in their encounter with Galatians.

I am grateful to many people for the writing of this text. First, I thank the community of faith that gathers at South Congregational Church, United Church of Christ, in Centerville, Massachusetts.[4] Many of my thoughts were formulated in preparation and response to the Sunday morning and Tuesday noon Bible studies. I am grateful to this historic white-steeple Cape Cod congregation for supporting my integration of pastoral ministry and theological reflection. I am also grateful to creative New Testament scholars Greg Carey and Ronald Farmer for their insights. Jody and Henry Neufeld at Energion Publications have been supportive of my work and have improved this text by their editorial comments.

I give thanks for pastors who have shaped my own vocation as a scholar-pastor – in particular, John Akers, Ernie Campbell, George Tolman, George "Shorty" Collins, Clayton Gooden – as well as teachers whose pastoral care enabled me to claim my role as a pastoral theologian – John Cobb, Marie Fox, David Griffin, Jack Verheyden, and Richard Keady. As always I give thanks for the companion of lifetime, Kate Gould Epperly, whose ministerial vocation has shaped the evolution of my own life as a scholar, pastor, spiritual guide, parent, and now grandparent of two small boys.

---

4   http://southcongregationalchurch-centerville.org/

BECOMING GALATIAN: SPIRITUAL PRACTICES FOR READING GALATIANS

If you open your spirit to God's wisdom, reading Galatians can set you free. For Paul, Jesus is all about freedom. "For freedom Christ has set us free. Stand firm, therefore, and do not submit again to a yoke of slavery" (5:1). Freedom, however, carries with it responsibility and is grounded in the movements of the God's Spirit in our lives. Grace comes through many sources – mystical experiences, providential encounters, dreams and intuitions, meditating on scripture, spiritual direction and counseling, theological reflection, social concern and compassionate action, and worship in the community of faith. Grace comes to us freely and without conditions. Grace can transform a persecutor into a proclaimer. Surprising grace saved the apostle Paul. But experiencing God's freely given grace often is the result of our opening ourselves to God's providential movements in our lives through spiritual practices, such as prayer, meditation, silence, holy reading, and sacred imagination. All of these practices enable us to experience the Bible as a living document rather than a dead word or source of theological and ethical contention. These practices enable us to discover that we are always on holy ground, living in a world where we can experience Christ on our personal road to Damascus or in every child's face.

The Bible can be read in many ways. We can read from an academic perspective. As I initially prepared for the Bible study on Galatians at South Congregational Church, I consulted the most insightful biblical scholars of our time. I also read Galatians in the original Greek to enhance my own appreciation for the nuances of translation. Moreover, I looked at several English translations as a way of understanding the multifaceted nature of the text and the underlying theological emphases of the translators. It may come as a surprise to the lay reader, but no biblical translation is fully objective or unbiased. Even the best of translators bring their own theological and spiritual perspective and experience to the text. This is not academic dishonesty, and most translators seek to be as unbiased as possible, but the recognition that our standpoint serves as the lens through which we view what happens in our lives, whether a car accident, chance encounter, diagnosis of cancer, or passage from scripture.

Galatians can also be read historically to discern the original audience and date of the text. A discerning reader will discover that there is no unanimous consensus about the date or audience of Paul's letter. It might have been written for the residents of the northern section of Galatia; it may also have been addressed to the emerging Christian communities in southern Galatia, Derbe, Lystra, and Iconium. It might have been written as early as 48 CE or as late as 55 CE. Historical and textual analysis helps us understand the culture, language, intentionality, occasion, and linguistic characteristics, formative of the Letter to the Galatians. An era before copyrights and computer stamping makes it difficult to have absolute certainty about the place, date, audience, and authorship of many books of the Bible.

Galatians may also be read as a source of Christian doctrine. This certainly was at the heart of Martin Luther's understanding of Galatians. Inspired by his own experience of God's freely-given and unmerited grace, Luther saw Galatians as the textbook of grace. Galatians served as one of the foundations of Luther's opposition to "works righteousness" as a way of earning salvation or putting oneself right with God. Luther believed that rituals, financial contributions (indulgences intended to buy our way out of purgatory), and legalistic practices – similar to the practice of circumcision,

Sabbath keeping, and kosher diets – can stand in the way of God's vision of salvation through the Cross of Christ.

All these approaches to scripture are important and we will explore each of these in the course of this study. But for most of us the ultimate meaning of scripture involves personal and social transformation and the practical application of scripture to the messiness of daily life. We read scripture so that its meaning might come alive in us and, like the communities gathered in Galatia, so that we might experience the Spirit of Christ as a lived reality and spiritual center of our lives. When we encounter scripture with heart, mind, and hands, the Bible comes alive and changes our lives and communities. We become the Galatians of our time, reveling in Christian freedom and living in the Spirit. We discover that God's liberating Word, incarnate in the crucified and risen Christ, challenges everything that gets in the way of spiritual freedom and faithful discipleship.

The spirit of Galatia is alive today, and it is just as controversial now as it was in the first century. Just a few weeks ago, the United States Supreme Court (October 2014) refused to reverse judicial decisions striking down bans of same sex marriage. Prior to that time, many gay and lesbian Christians experienced liberation in their encounter with Galatians' words: "there is no longer Jew or Greek, there is no longer slave or free, there is no longer male or female; for all are you are one in Christ Jesus"(3:28). On the other hand, many Christians believe that limiting the freedom of gay and lesbian persons to marry is consistent with a faithful reading of the scriptures. Just a few decades ago, Martin Luther King spoke of Sunday morning as the most segregated hour in America. No doubt he was inspired by Paul's own affirmation that in Galatia, and our time, "separate but equal" status in worship and fellowship leads to second-class status for Gentile, and twentieth century African American, Christians. We are the Galatians of our time, and we must always be on the lookout for practices that would threaten the freedom we have in Christ.

Practicing Galatians

It is my belief that we nurture the Galatian spirit best by encountering scripture through a variety of spiritual practices. These practices of grace enable scripture to come alive in heart, mind, and hands. Contemplative practices are not difficult. They are focused activities based on what we normally do each day – pausing, focusing, and responding to encounters and events in our environment. The challenge is doing these practices regularly and intentionally. Still, the reward of meditating on scripture and taking time for prayer and contemplation is great. If you commit yourself to these practices, you will experience the transformed mind that Paul describes in Romans 2:12. You may also find yourself embodying the mind of Christ in your daily interactions (Philippians 2:5, 1 Corinthians 2:16). In this section, we will explore how to experience God's Spirit, and indeed the mind of Christ, through what Brother Lawrence called "the practice of the presence of God" in your encounter with Paul's Letter to the Galatians.

Breathing with the Spirit. From the very beginning of history, breath has been identified with the spiritual energies of life. Hindus speak of this energy in terms of *prana.* Traditional Chinese medicine describes the energy of life as *chi.* The Hebrews spoke of *ruach* as God's animating breath, and the earliest Christians described the Holy Spirit as *pneuma,* the enlivening and empowering breath of God, blowing freely through human life and all creation. On Easter night, Jesus breathed on his followers, as they were gathered in an upper room, and said, "Receive the Holy Spirit" (John 20:22). Perhaps, thinking of Psalm 150:6, "let everything that breathes praise God," the apostle Paul speaks of the Spirit praying within us "in sighs too deep for words" (Romans 8:26).

Intentional breathing as a spiritual practice calms and centers, and connects us with divine wisdom. I often begin a bible study or prayer group with the suggestion that members take a moment to pause in God's presence, breathing in God's wisdom as they prepare to study God's words for us. I use this same practice to open my spirit to divine wisdom in my own personal study and reflection on scripture. A breath prayer I have come to use goes as follows:

I inhale God's wisdom.
I exhale God's blessing.

Another breath prayer I learned nearly forty years ago from retired Congregational pastor Allan Armstrong Hunter:

I breathe the spirit deeply in
And blow it joyfully out again.

The global perspective encouraged by Paul's Letter to the Galatians invites us to listen to another breath prayer, articulated by Vietnamese Buddhist Monk Thich Nhat Hanh:

Breathing in I feel calm.
Breathing out I smile.

Based on Psalm 150:6, I often say the following, "Every breath a prayer; every breath a blessing," as a reminder that God is as near as my next breath and that my spiritual practices shape my relationships with others. Whether you read Galatians individually or in a group, take time to embody Paul's affirmation that God's Spirit speaks within us, saying "Abba, Father," through moments of silent breathing as you begin your study.

Holy Reading. God is constantly inspiring us. Moment by moment, God's Spirit provides us with insights, inspirations, and visions of possibility. When we encounter scripture prayerfully, it becomes a living word, able to speak to our current situation. In Galatians, Paul assumes that scripture is a living document, whose meaning is constantly changing, depending on our life situation. Like a good friend or parent, God's words to humanity do not remain static and unchanging, but reflect God's constancy in new and creative ways. This surely is the meaning of Lamentations 3:22-23:

The steadfast love of the Lord never ceases,
his mercies never come to an end;
they are new every morning;
great is your faithfulness.

Two thousand years after the writing of Lamentations, John Robinson (1576-1625), one of the pastoral leaders of the American Pilgrim fathers and mothers, asserted: "for I am verily persuaded the Lord hath more truth and light yet to break forth from His holy word."

Paul believes that more light can be shed on the scriptures, especially the understanding of the covenant with Abraham and Sarah. Words that were used to separate Jews and Gentiles were reinterpreted by Paul to express God's covenant with all peoples. Perhaps Paul's imaginative approach to scripture inspired the work of Benedict of Narsia, the founder of the Benedictine Order, who developed the practice of *lectio divina,* or holy reading, as a way to experience scripture as a source of personal and community wisdom. Traditionally, the practice of holy reading has four steps, although you may wish to abbreviate it in your Bible study. You can spend five minutes or five hours meditating on the word and wisdom of a passage from scripture or other literature through *lectio divina.*[5]

1) *Prayerful Reading.* The first step in *lectio divina* is simply to read the text slowly and meditatively. You may even choose to read it orally, so you might hear the words aloud like the first listeners among the communities of Galatia. Savor the words as if you are hearing them for the first time. Don't try to analyze the text or fit it into your previous understandings of God or Christian faith, but open to God's inspiration in this moment, with as few theological

---

5   For more on the Benedictine spiritual path, see Norvene Vest, *Preferring Christ: A Devotional Commentary on the Rule of St. Benedict* (New York:Morehouse Press, 2004) and Kathleen Norris, *Cloister Walk* (New York: Riverhead Books, 1997).

biases as possible. God is still speaking and creating in our lives, and new understandings of scripture can emerge at any time. Participatory Bible study involves your commitment seeing scripture as a living word, becoming a companion with the scripture, and letting it shape your experience of the world in the here and now.

2) *Meditating on the Words.* The second step in holy reading involves listening for the words that speak personally and directly to you today. What words, phrases, or images stand out in your reading? What words, phrases, or images console or inspire? What words, phrases, or images trouble or convict you? If you are studying Galatians in a group, you will discover the many ways people can experience the same passage. This reminds us that there is a democracy of revelation in which God addresses us where we are, as persons and communities. Each person, including you, is touched by God in a saving and illuminating way and can bring something to our understanding of the text. In addition, this process challenges us to recognize that there are many authentic ways to encounter scripture and that God does not desire uniformity in experience, worship, or theology. God has a personal word for you, for other persons, and for the many Christian communities. One thing you may discover as you read Galatians is that even in the beginnings of the Christian movement, people had very different understandings of Jesus' message and what it meant to be a follower of Jesus. As you consider today's spiritual landscape, you will discover the variety of ways that Christians have understood the sacraments of the church or the relationship between grace and human effort, reflected in today's historic denominations and emerging communities.

3) *Praying the Words.* Prayerfully allow a particular phrase, or image to soak deeply into your experience. You may

choose to repeat the word over and over again, or reflect on its meaning for you today. You may also choose to compose a prayer or question addressed to God, based on your encounter with the text. Nothing is off limits in our prayer lives. God wants us to share our whole selves in prayer. In so doing, we come to know ourselves in our grandeur and weakness as well as God's mercies and challenges to us.

4) *Contemplating the Words.* Holy reading calls us to go deeper in our experience of God's personal and creative word in the words of scripture. In contemplation, we choose to listen and then let God speak to us in silence as well as the spoken word. In the midst of busy day, we may heed the words of the Psalmist, "be still and know that I am God" (Psalm 46:10). God who speaks in sighs too deep for words (Romans 8:26) is constantly inspiring us, speaking to us through scripture, hunches and intuitions, unexpected inspirations, and our daily encounters. While revelation may come as a matter of grace and surprise, we can also prepare to experience divine wisdom when it emerges in the course of the day.

This four step process is often best done in personal or community retreat settings. I have, however, adapted the practice of *lectio divina* to group bible study or prayer/meditation settings group, occurring within the parameter of forty-five minutes to an hour. I follow a simple practice of reading the scripture twice with a short pause in between. I read slowly and deliberately, allowing the listener to follow along. After the second reading, the group takes between three to five minutes to encounter the text in stillness, listening for the word or image that emerges in each participant's experience. Following this, we take a few minutes for group conversation, sharing as each feels called the wisdom he or she has experienced. Often, the insights from this brief time of holy reading shape the rest of the bible study or prayer/meditation group.[6]

Holy Imagination. God is profoundly imaginative and creative. God has given us the gift of creativity. Yet, many of us let the well-springs of imagination dry up as we grow older. In the words of J.B. Phillips' translation of Romans 12:2, we have allowed the world to squeeze us into its mold.

One way to read Galatians or any other biblical text is to let the text inspire your imagination. This approach, which has become popular in guided visualizations and imaginative prayers, is at the heart of biblical tales such as the legends of Job and Esther and Jesus' parables. Jesus invited his listeners to imagine what it would be like to be a lost sheep or to go in search of a lost sheep on a dark night. He asked his disciples to imagine how they would feel, and what they would do, if they found a buried treasure or lost a precious coin. He asked them to consider the relationship of a father and his two sons, and the joy of welcoming a wayward child home.

Ignatius of Loyola, the founder of the Roman Catholic order, the Society of Jesus or Jesuits (1491-1556), suggested that people use their imagination to find the deeper meaning of scripture.[7] They might, for example, imagine what it would be like to be Adam and Eve rejoicing in the beauty of the primordial garden and then yielding to temptation and discovering their nakedness before God and each other. A person might identify with the male disciples or Jesus' mother and his female followers watching the crucifixion of Jesus, by noting the scene, the crowd gathered at the cross, and your own feelings as you watched the Romans crucify your teacher and savior. Which of these observers do you most identify with? How do you feel as you see your teacher and friend being crucified? How might an opponent such as Pilate respond to the consequences of his decision?

---

6   Much of this chapter is adapted from *Philippians: A Participatory Study Guide* (Gonzalez, FL: Energion Publications, 2011).

7   David Fleming, *The Spiritual Exercises of St. Ignatius of Loyola: A Literal Translation and Contemporary Reading* (Institute of Jesuit Studies), 1978.

While the Letter to the Galatians doesn't contain parables, you might enter Paul's study as he wrote his passionate response to the situation in Galatian communities. You might imagine Paul challenging Peter over dietary rules and table fellowship with Gentiles. You might experience the world from the viewpoint of a Gentile Christian as he or she experiences the intoxicating nature of freedom and then has second thoughts about life without chains. In imaginatively exploring the encounter of Peter and Paul, as recorded in Galatians, you might ponder the following and then visualize the event: What words did Peter and Paul exchange? How did Peter justify his changed behavior toward the Gentile Christians? What feelings of ambivalence shaped the Galatians response to their new found freedom? How did the onlookers feel as they witnessed this passionate disagreement between two spiritual authorities?

We are the Galatians of our time and Paul's letter comes alive, revealing our own spiritual challenges and potential to retreat from freedom or deny freedom to others, when we embrace the text as our story and not just words addressed to an ancient community.

The Power of Affirmative Faith. The Bible is a book of affirmations that can change your life and transform the world. Paul proclaims, "Do not be conformed to this world but be transformed by the renewing of your mind" (Romans 12:2). This "world" can take on many meanings, one of which involves our tendency to negativity, self-limitation, and polarization. In Philippians, Paul tells us to "think about these things" (4:8), that is, to focus on what is honorable, pure, and pleasing. In so doing, Paul is inviting us to embody an affirmative faith by using short phrases to reshape our vision of the world. Spiritual affirmations are statements, positively stated in the present tense, that describe our deepest reality as God's beloved children.

Many of us are shaped by negative self-talk. Consider the following questions as a catalyst for self-examination: What negative self-talk characterizes your life? What limiting statements do you say to yourself? For example, I've heard people make the following negative statements about themselves. I've even said a few of them myself. Such statements reveal our sense of inadequacy and inability to live out our vocation as God's children.

- ✓ I'm too old to change.
- ✓ I'm not talented enough.
- ✓ I'm not intelligent enough, healthy enough, or skilled enough.
- ✓ I'll never find someone that loves me.
- ✓ I'm too fat, too short, too bald, or too ugly, for anyone to love me.
- ✓ I don't have enough time, money, or resources, to succeed.
- ✓ I am a sinner and unworthy of God's love.
- ✓ I'll never receive the recognition in my field or workplace that I deserve.

Our negative self-talk places limits on our lives and our expectations. Sadly, these self-limiting and negative statements often shape our economic well-being, self-esteem, and physical health.

Paul's letter to the Galatians contains some of the most powerful and life-transforming affirmative prayers. Paul challenges his Galatian listeners and us to live by the following affirmations about God and us.

- ✓ God's grace sets me free. (Galatians 2:4)
- ✓ Christ lives in me. (Galatians 2:20)
- ✓ In Christ, I am redeemed and freed from the past. (Galatians 3:13)
- ✓ We are one in Christ. (Galatians 3:28)
- ✓ All are persons are beloved and equal as brothers and sisters in Christ. (Galatians 3:28)
- ✓ Christ sets me free. (Galatians 5:1)
- ✓ I live by God's Spirit. (Galatians 5:25)
- ✓ In Christ I am a new creation. (Galatians 6:15)

Galatians is a testimony to God's love for us. The Cross witnesses to God's willingness to suffer to free us from the bondage of sin, negativity, and injustice. God wants us to have abundant life in body, mind, spirit, and relationships (John 10:10). Affirmations transform our perspective on the world and ourselves and enable us to claim God's willingness to give us more than we can ask or imagine (Ephesians 3:20).

Affirmations challenge us to move from passive acceptance of injustice and mediocrity to intentional agency to bring health, beauty, and love to the world. They remind us that because "nothing can separate us from the love of God" (Romans 8:38-39), we can claim our vocation as "the light of the world" (Matthew 5:14).

Circling the Text. Often when I lead a Bible study, I provide the participants with a photocopy of the text we are studying. I invite them to take a few moments for silence and then slowly read the text, circling the words that are most meaningful to them. I used this approach recently with my confirmation class at South Congregational Church as a way of reflecting on the theme of God, creation, and science. Needless to say, we had a free-spirited and provocative discussion.

The Great "What If?" An imaginative reading of scripture always involves exploring alternative possibilities and the roads not taken in the early church. Scripture is full of "what if's." As you read Galatians, you might explore the following "what if" possibilities:

- ✓ What if ... the Jerusalem leaders of the Jesus movement had not approved Paul's vision of full participation of Gentiles?
- ✓ What if ... the more conservative and traditionalist movement had won the debate over requiring Gentiles to

live according to Jewish law (diet, circumcision, Sabbath-keeping)?

✓ What if … we had at our disposal and could read documents or hear speeches from the more conservative and traditionalist members of the Jesus movement?

✓ What if … we could have heard Peter's response to Paul?

✓ What if … the Christian movement had remained, for all intents and purposes, a Jewish sect rather than a multicultural movement? How would this have changed the world?

Even though Paul appears to have won the battle at Galatia – after all, Galatians became part of the authoritative Christian scriptures – his controversy with the traditionalist movement testifies to diversity in theology and practice within the early Christian movement. It reminds us that today's Christian movement is dynamic and multifaceted. There is no one pathway ahead for us individually, for our congregations, or for our denomination. As I write, Pope Francis is presenting today's Roman Catholic Church with an array of provocative possibilities that would not have been entertained if another leader had been chosen. Within the Protestant family in North America, many denominations are trying to respond faithfully to their gay and lesbian members, pastors, and seminarians as well as issues of responding to immigration and global climate change. Many pathways are possible, each of which leads to further adventures in following Jesus.

So What! While Paul's theology is often contrasted with the Letter of James, both Christian leaders believed that faith without works is dead (James 5:17).[8] Paul affirms "the only thing that counts is faith working through love" (5:6). A living faith joins contemplation and action, and theology and practices. Our beliefs shape our overall well-being and inspire us to action so that God's

---

8 For more on the Letter of James, see Bruce Epperly, *Holistic Spirituality: Life Giving Wisdom from the Letter of James* (Gonzalez, FL: Energion Publications, 2014).

realm might come on earth as it is in heaven. As you read Galatians, consider the practical implications of the various theological statements made by the apostle Paul:

✓ If Gentiles and Jews are equals before God, how does this change their behavior in church and the world?
✓ If Jew and Greek, slave and free, and male and female are one in Christ, how might this have influenced the political and economic actions of the early Christian movement? How might it influence our own ethics and congregational decision-making?
✓ What "sacred cows" is Paul challenging in the Letter to the Galatians? What "sacred cows" do we need to challenge to be faithful to God in our time?

A living word is always practical and sometimes political and economic. Paul and his fellow Christians had no political power in the Roman empire and did not endeavor, as objects of persecution, to shape public policy. But whatever shapes our spiritual lives also shapes pocketbook issues and the scope of our concern for neighbors and strangers.

CONCLUDING WORDS

All of these exercises may be integrated and adapted to your particular group Bible study context. In addition to these exercises, I have included a list of questions to conclude each section. Once again, feel free to adapt these to your setting and devise other questions for reflection. The Bible comes alive when it addresses us as a personal word, and not an abstract concept, unrelated to our individual, congregational, and community setting.

Introduction And Background

Galatians 1:1-10

Vision

Participants will gain a basic understanding of the authorship, date, and setting of the Letter to Galatians. They will reflect on the uniqueness of Paul's Letter to the Galatians, the issues at stake, and the reasons for Paul's urgency. Participants will consider the nature of scripture as a living word in terms of its interpretation as well as its meaning for us today. Central to our study is the recognition that we are still responding to the issues faced by the Galatian community, especially as these relate to the interplay of unity, diversity, and equality in the church.

Opening Prayer

God is constantly speaking a liberating word to us. Yet, like the Christian communities in Galatia, we are tempted to backslide into familiar and dysfunctional habits. Prayer is never about preserving the status quo or returning to an irrelevant past. Whether in individual or group settings, prayer connects us with the communion of saints, embodied in what Jaraslov Pelikan referred to as "the living thoughts of dead people," as well as God's new creation in this moment of time. Prayer is the ultimate act of connection with God, our deeper selves, and those around us.

Begin with a generous time of stillness, opening prayerfully to God's Spirit with each calming and centering breath. Experience the fullness of God's silence expressing itself in sighs too deep for words.

Holy One, you speak a living word to us in the words of scripture. Help us to discover new insights in ancient wisdom. As we read Paul's words to communities of a past era, help us to claim our own living experience of Christ and discover the new creation that God promises us in Jesus' name. Amen.

Paul As Evangelist, Theologian, And Spiritual Guide (1:1-3)

Marcus Borg and John Dominic Crossan speak of three Pauls – the revolutionary, the conservative, and the reactionary. If their analysis is accurate, Galatians is a revolutionary document. The freedom that comes from a personal relationship with the crucified and risen Christ is at the heart of Paul's message. In the cross and resurrection, Christ liberates us from the bondage of sin and external authority and opens us to God's liberating spirit, whose inner presence guides, inspires, corrects, and challenges individuals and communities alike. Although the Spirit inspires us to cry out "Abba, Father," God's personal presence is always global as well as individual. As Paul was to say to another troubled Christian community, we are all interconnected members of the body of Christ. Our individual spiritual well-being contributes to the well-being of the community and the well-being of the community brings forth spiritually healthy persons. The "mind of Christ" moves through and inspires the body – the faith community - as a whole and each individual part (1 Corinthians 12:12-31; Philippians 2:5-11).

Paul's witness to the living Christ emerges from a mystical experience on the road to Damascus in which Saul the persecutor of the Jesus movement becomes the Paul proclaimer of Christ's salvation for all (Acts 9:1-9). A teacher and rigorous follower of the Law of Moses, Paul feels compelled to silence the followers of the growing Jesus movement. Acting as a type of religious district attorney, with the authority to arrest members of this heretical movement, Paul travels to Damascus. On the way, Jesus comes to him in a blinding light, challenging his religious orthodoxy, and giving him the commission of apostle to the Gentiles. Paul's Damascus Road experience is not purely subjective, but the result of encountering the Risen Christ, whose energy and power now becomes Paul's guiding light and spiritual center. Mysticism leads to mission as Paul discovers that he has been "sent" by God to share God's good news.

After a time of reflection, Paul sets out to share the good news in the Mediterranean world. Although he no doubt shares the message of the crucified and risen Christ with Jews on the way, his mandate from God and the Jerusalem church is to spread the gospel to the Gentile world. Driven by Christ's spirit, Paul risks life and limb to share the message in places such as Rome, Ephesus, Philippi, Galatia, and Corinth.

As I stated earlier, Paul's letters reveal a religion in the making. Despite his protests otherwise, no doubt Paul received instruction in the faith, perhaps from Ananias and others (see Acts 9:10-20). But, we can suspect that Paul's own message was a creative synthesis of his mystical encounter with Christ, his personal autobiography, and the oral traditions surrounding Jesus. In many ways, the theology that Paul preaches through his letters to emerging Christian communities is parallel to the Gospel of John in form, though not necessarily content. Whereas Matthew and Luke begin their gospels with the birth of the Messiah, and the wondrous events of angelic visitations, dreams, unexpected births, and magi, John begins with metaphysics, proclaiming that the word made flesh reflects the creative world-creating wisdom of God (John 1:1-5, 9). Paul also waxes metaphysical in his affirmation that Jesus Christ is more than a man; he reveals the heart and mind of God, evident both in our salvation and in the formation of the cosmos. Paul's Christ is both global and personal, and untethered from the geography of Galilee. Although Paul was no doubt aware of the stories of Jesus' birth, the parables, and the events of his life, his Messiah is known by the interplay of suffering and triumph. Throughout his writings, Paul says nothing about the virgin birth and Jesus' message. Still, the message of radical inclusion we find in Galatians and Paul's other letters embodies Jesus' ministry of radical hospitality. The crucified and risen one is also the one who accepted sinners, embraced women and outcasts, shared good news beyond his ethnic group, and opened his followers to God's new creation. This is Paul's message as well.

Paul's words in Galatia helped shape future Christian theology. Written twenty to fifty years before the four gospels and perhaps twenty years after Christ's ascension into heaven, Paul defines the Christian movement enabling it to become a global religion, transcending ethnicity and culture.[9] Paul's spiritual vision was, as Galatians clearly shows, but one of the options available to early followers of Jesus. Paul's passionate words in Galatians are addressed to fellow Christians for whom ethnicity trumps grace, and following the law eclipses spiritual liberation.

Paul eventually won the day – Galatians became part of the new movement's sacred writings. The only recollections we have of Paul's opponents come from Paul's own hand. What would have happened if Paul's Letter to the Galatians had been lost? What would have been the shape of Christianity if Paul's opponents had triumphed? As I ponder these mysteries, I wonder whether a Western church would have emerged and my own congregation would have existed if Paul's message had not be preserved and later included in the New Testament. I wonder whether I would have even known about the message of Jesus. In the intricate ecology of the history of Christianity, Paul is, for good or for ill, one of the shapers of Christian theology and also Western civilization and global Christianity, and in Galatians we find the seeds of a movement that now encompasses over two billion persons. As I consider

---

9   Most scholars believe the Letter to the Galatians was written between 48 and 53 CE. The dating of the gospels ranges from as early at 65-75 CE (Mark) and as late as 100-110 CE (John).

the impact of Galatians on the future of Christianity, I believe that your reading this book is ultimately the result of Paul's influence, and in particular, his message to the churches in Galatia.

Who Are the Galatians? (1:2)

Today, when I make a pastoral call on Cape Cod or take a trip to Boston or elsewhere to give a talk or sightsee, I consult Mapquest or Google Maps. I also have a GPS on my phone that usually points me in the right direction and can be used to by myself and others to pinpoint my exact location. Those who study Paul's original writings do not have such luxuries. Time and place are vague in the Biblical stories. Paul's greeting is addressed to "the churches in Galatia" (1:2). But which Galatia is the apostle talking about? The province of Galatia included most of central Turkey at the time of Paul's ministry. The citizens of Galatia were of Celtic ethnicity, the descendants of tribes that moved southward to today's Turkey and northward to contemporary France, England, Ireland and Scotland. That's where our certainty ends. Could Paul's letter have been written to Christian communities in northern Galatia or the more southerly communities described in Acts 14:1-23, Iconium, Lystra, and Derbe?

Acts 14 describes Paul's memorable visit to southern Galatia. In the course of preaching the good news of the crucified and risen Christ, Paul and Barnabas were stoned, fled for their lives, healed a paralyzed man, were identified as gods, and proclaimed God's grace to all peoples. Paul's vision of God goes beyond the Jewish tradition: "God has not left himself without a witness in doing good – giving you rain from heaven and fruitful seasons, and filling you with food and your hearts with joy" (Acts 14:12). At every step of the way, Paul and Barnabas are confronted by Jewish opponents, who incite violence against them. When Paul and Silas finally depart from Galatia for their home base in Antioch, Syria, they appoint elders as spiritual leaders of the newly founded faith communities, whose task is to continue the good work God has begun in their churches.

Sometime after he returns to Antioch, Paul hears that issues of ethnicity and faith are troubling the Galatian congregations. His message of liberation and equality has been challenged, as we shall see, by a group of Christian teachers, preaching a traditionalist message, joining the teachings of Jesus with the requirement to embrace of Jewish culture and ritual as essential to experience the fullness of God's grace. The exact date of this controversy and Paul's initial response to it, recorded in Galatians, is unknown. Scholars date Paul's letter as early as 48 CE and as late as 55 CE. While knowing the date of Paul's writing is not crucial for our understanding of the letter today, the vagueness of place and date cautions us to be humble in our quest to understand the Letter to the Galatians and the Bible as a whole.

Paul's Words of Greeting (1:1-5)

In our age of immediate communication by phone, electronic mail, texting, or social media, the art of letter writing has been lost. In earlier times, writing a letter was a contemplative practice, often revealing the soul of the writer to her or his listeners. Writing took a great deal of effort and was accomplished by the slow movement of ink on parchment. This was true of Paul's letters to early Christian congregations. We can imagine Paul ruminating over the words he was planning to share to the Galatians and then dictating them to his secretary. The scarcity of writing materials made revisions difficult so the author had to be clear about sharing her or his wisdom.

In the case of the Letter to the Galatians, Paul is covering new theological ground. He may even be on the verge of "inventing" Christian theology. He is trying to constellate his message in short form. There is urgency in his tone that precludes calm and contemplative conversation. The community is in crisis and he must step in if his understanding of the gospel and the mission to the Gentiles is to survive. His words are strong and passionate, and we wonder if he had second thoughts about some of his phrasing once the letter was delivered to the churches in Galatia. Still, fallible as the Galatian letter was, it has stood has stood the test of time, providing insight into the formation of the Jesus movement and shaping our understandings of grace, law, salvation, and the cross.

Paul begins the letter by sharing his credentials and authority as a leader of the earlier church. Listen to his first words, "Paul, an apostle sent neither by human commission or human authorities, but from Jesus Christ and God the father" (1:1). Paul's phrasing is not accidental. He is establishing his apostolic authority, equal to that of Peter and James, the brother of Jesus, and leader of the Jerusalem church, at that time the center of the Christian movement. An apostle is a messenger and Paul's message comes straight from God. While he did not know Jesus in the flesh with the same intimacy as his earthly disciples, his knowledge of Christ, mystical calling as an apostle, and spiritual power came from his mystical encounter with Jesus on the road to Damascus.

Scholars believe that those whom I describe as the "apostles of tradition" not only questioned Paul's liberating message but his authority to speak for Christ to begin with. In Paul's mind, message and messenger are inseparable. He cannot separate his mystical encounter from his calling to preach good news to the Gentiles. When other Christians question his message, Paul believes that they are questioning God's intentions for humankind.

In today's postmodern context, Paul's affirmation begs the questions: Doesn't revelation require a receiver, whose life experiences and culture shape the message? Is Paul's gospel both a revelation from God and a revealing of Paul's own personal struggles with law and grace? If God personally addresses each of us, are Paul's words intended to be universal in scope or are they limited to a particular time and place? These are difficult questions. Still, I believe that while Paul's experience of the risen Christ was personal and local, and thus to some extent limited and relative to his situation, his words contain a truth that echoes through the centuries describing our own quest for freedom from the past and liberation from the constraints of legalism. Through God's gentle providence, Paul's words struck a chord in Galatia and have continued to do so throughout the ages.

Paul continues, in his traditional form, to bless his listeners with "grace and peace." Though this greeting is commonplace, the grace that he pronounces comes from God and from Jesus Christ, "who gave himself for our sins to set us free from the present evil age" (1:4). In these words we have an early theory of atonement in miniature. Christ's sacrifice liberates humankind from all that would destroy and oppress us. We live in an "evil age," Paul contends, in which we must struggle with personal guilt and imperfection as well as persecution, conflict, and temptation. As a Jew, Paul's faith is this-worldly and is reflected in the affirmation that God's creative wisdom that brings forth life in all its wondrous variety and beauty. He is equally sure that human imperfection, dare we call it sin, has ruptured God's intended vision – the realm of Shalom – for humankind and all earthly creation. This present age is the complex and confusing – beautiful yet flawed, God-filled yet disobedient. We know this same ambiguity on a daily basis. We celebrate the beauty of the earth, but mourn the death of a child from cancer or a teen in an altercation with a police officer.

As he writes to the Galatians, Paul is holding two thoughts in tension – the goodness of creation and human life and the tragic realities of human decision-making at the personal and corporate level. As I write these words in November 2014, in some quarters there is near panic, inflamed by the news media, about an Ebola epidemic; Syria and Iraq are in shambles and terrorists are beheading journalists and persons deemed infidels, including the ancient communities in Antioch and Chaldea; lone gunmen massacre friends; political polarization abounds in an election year; a young man has been killed in Ferguson, Missouri, causing racial tension and reopening the wounds of racism and alienation in the body politic; and the gap between the wealthy and the poor increases each day. My morning walk on the beaches of Cape Cod is marred by worries about my professional and economic future, the future of the congregation I pastor, and threats of global warming and terrorist attacks. Often I feel powerless to change anything, including my own personal challenges.

Paul's words gave the Galatians hope for transformation and they are hopeful to us, too. Jesus Christ frees us from bondage. The external world may not immediately change, but the cross and resurrection of Jesus Christ frees us from guilt, fear, anxiety, and hopelessness. God acts in Christ to set us free to live joyfully and creatively. The cross and resurrection are a matter of life and death – they must be proclaimed – spiritually, ethically, and communally. Anything that challenges God's liberating message must be confronted boldly.

A Greeting That Challenges And Convicts (1:6-10)

After his initial salutation to the church at Philippi, Paul continues with "I thank God every time I remember you, praying with joy in every one of my prayers for all of you, because of your sharing of the gospel from the first day until now" (Philippians 1:3). Contrast this with Paul's personal word to the churches in Galatia: "I am astonished that you are so quickly deserting the one who called you in the grace of Christ and are turning to a different gospel" (1:6). While Paul exhibits no lack of care for the spiritual well-being of the Galatian communities, he is amazed and angry at their fall from grace. Paul's first listeners knew that they were in for a theological and spiritual tongue lashing in the words to come.

Paul speaks of a different gospel. Unfortunately, we don't know the objects of Paul's ire. No doubt they are Christians, followers of the same Jesus as Paul and the Galatian Christians; but Paul believes that their message is subverting his authority and perverting the freely given good news of God's unmerited grace. Scholars believe that the early church had many diverse streams of theology and spirituality. Some scholars suggest that following Paul's missionary visit to Galatia, other evangelists preached to the Galatian communities. These evangelists, perhaps emissaries from James the brother of Jesus and leader of the Jerusalem church, taught a more conservative and traditional gospel. They no doubt affirmed their common faith with Paul that Jesus was Savior and Lord, but they saw a significant deficiency in Paul's message. Paul focused on the freedom of Christ and Christ's overcoming of ethnic and cultural differences. Paul did not require his Gentiles to adopt Jewish practices in order to follow Jesus. In contrast, Paul's critics asserted that to become a full-fledged follower of Jesus, the Gentiles had to adopt Jewish dietary practices and holy days, and if they were males, they needed be circumcised as a sign of their fidelity to God.

In the process of teaching the necessity of following Jewish practices to be a full-fledged follower of Jesus, these evangelists apparently had a "yes-but" attitude toward Paul and his message. "Yes, Paul is preaching the good news of the crucified and risen Jesus, but Paul's message is incomplete. Paul forgot the importance of tradition. To be a follower of Jesus you have to adopt his Jewish lifestyle and religious practices." Some may have added, "Paul is devout and faithful, but he never encountered Jesus in the flesh. He doesn't have the authority or insight of James or Peter." Again, it is unfortunate that Paul's opponents can't speak for themselves. Their message in their own words has been lost, and all we have is Paul's passionate denunciation.

Fueled by his passionate commitment to God's grace, Paul curses those who preach a different gospel. He condemns their message as a false gospel. In fact, to Paul, they have no gospel – no good news – because their message is filled with requirements necessary to earn God's love. In the defense of Paul's critics, we must affirm that their intention was not malevolent. They too preached the gospel in good faith, sharing their understanding of Christ, according to their theological orientation. As we will see, the issues at stake involve the dynamics and tension of tradition and novelty and law and freedom. Just as important, in light of the historical realities of Christian imperialism, is Paul's opponents' belief in the necessity of the Galatians and any other foreign, usually non-Western, people to repudiate their culture to follow Jesus. Paul's denunciation of his critics reflects his love for his Gentile communities. He is affirming that you can be a follower of Jesus and live according to the practices of your own culture. Jew and Gentile are equal before God, and Gentiles do not have to become Jews to follow Jesus. Christian history would have been radically different had Jesus' followers taken Paul's message of Christian equality to heart in their relationships with indigenous people in North and South America, Africa, and Asia.

Paul's diatribe begs the question of diversity within the faith community. Are there strict norms for following Jesus, culturally, theologically, or ritually? How much diversity can we affirm without putting the essentials of our faith in jeopardy? Can we have different "gospels," that is, understandings of Jesus, worship, God's relationship to humankind, or the varieties of human expression and still affirm Christian unity? These are not yesterday's questions. They have surfaced in the culture wars among Christians related to science and scripture, the ordination of women, and the acceptance of gay and lesbian persons as full Christians, worthy of ordination into ministry.

Questions for Discussion

1) As we encounter the Letter to the Galatians, we are reading a letter that Paul never intended us to read. In fact, Paul had no idea that his words would become part of today's New Testament. Consider the writings of other spiritual teachers, for example, your pastors through the years. What was their reason for writing to the congregation? What themes were important to them? If you were to write a letter to your congregation what would its focus be?

2) Today, the Letter to the Galatians carries the authority of scripture. It is considered to be the word and wisdom of God, or divine revelation to humankind. How can letters to people no longer alive be "revelation" to us? Does rev-

elation exclude imperfection? Do we have to treat every word of Galatians and the scriptures as equally revealing of God's vision for humankind and the church?

3)   Read Galatians 1:1-10 as a whole. What do you think of Paul's change in tone at verse 1:6? How would you feel if your pastor or another religious leader spoke to you in the way that Paul did to the Galatians? Putting yourself in the shoes of the Galatians, how do you think they initially responded to Paul's words?

4)   Take time to read the first few verses of Paul's letters to the Philippians and Ephesians along with his greeting in Galatians. How are they similar? How do they differ? What does this tell you about Paul's state of mind and the situation in Galatia?

5)   Paul describes himself as an "apostle" (1:1)? What is the meaning of the word "apostle?" On what does Paul base his authority? Do you think everyone appreciated or affirmed Paul's self-designation?

6)   Paul's salutation contains the words, "Grace to you and peace from God our Father and the Lord Jesus Christ" (1:3). Grace is at the heart of the Letter to the Galatians. What does grace mean to you? What is the peace that God gives us?

7)   Paul affirms that Jesus Christ "gave himself for our sins to set us free from the present evil age." Paul's words represent an early statement of the atonement theory, the way that Christ reconciles or restores our unity with God." What images of atonement – God's process of salvation - are present in this passage? What do you think Paul means by "the present evil age?" How might the Galatians have understood Christ's liberating work? How might it have transformed their lives?

8)   Why is it important for Paul to claim that his calling came through Jesus Christ, and not a human authority? How is the source of his authority different from the others (1:1,

read ahead to 1:11-12)? What do you think of persons who claim that they are speaking as a result of God's call without an intermediary? When you hear someone say "God told me" or "the Spirit revealed this to me," what is your response? How do we judge the veracity and insight of their revelation?

9) Paul's argument is with other Christians, who challenge his theological understanding and authority as an apostle. What is the "different" gospel, which is to Paul no gospel? Can there be two or more gospel messages? What invalidates this other gospel in Paul's mind? How shall we deal with competing truth claims? Is it possible to have too much diversity? How do we balance the reality of pluralism, the affirmation of many pathways of truth and salvation or many ways to be a Christian, with our quest for truth (1:4-9)?

10) We don't fully know the identity those who challenged Paul's theological views and authority. Are there any problems inherent in trusting Paul's description of their position to be accurate? Do you think we would have had a better understanding of Galatians if we had their side of the story? What do you think of Paul's "curse" on those who follow a different type of Christianity? How is this curse helpful or harmful to the cause of Christ?

11) Imaginatively construct a dialogue from Paul's opponents. What would the main points of their speeches be?

Closing Prayer

Loving God, give us open minds and hearts as we encounter the wondrous diversity of creation and humankind. Help us look more deeply into our brothers and sisters, honoring their uniqueness even as we affirm our own unique gifts. In Jesus' name. Amen.

Chosen by God

Galatians 1:11-24

Vision

In this section, participants will hear Paul describe his encounter with Christ as the source of his apostolic authority. Participants will reflect on the nature of revelation and mystical experiences as well as the variety of ways people can encounter God. Although Paul asserts that his vocation and authority as an apostle emerged from his own experience and not the teachings of other Christian leaders, participants will reflect on whether or not our experiences are sufficient as a source of spiritual authority and wisdom.

Prayer

Prayer is a form of connection between God, us, and others. Prayer affirms that we are all in this together. When we pray for others, we create a positive field of force around them, enabling God to be more effective in their lives.

Let us begin our prayer time with silence, breathing deeply and slowly, centering on God's presence in our lives. Take a moment in the silence to pray for the people in the group, asking God to bless them with insight and well-being.

Holy One, awaken us to you holy light as we go about our daily business. Help us to experience your presence in the subtle as well as dramatic moments of life. Let every encounter be a prayer and every word be a blessing as we attend to your word and wisdom. In Christ's Name. Amen.

Paul's Mysticism (1:11-24)

Once again, we return to the subject of religious experience and the many ways we can encounter God. To understand Galatians 1:11-24, we need to read imaginatively the account of Paul's spiritual transformation as recorded in Acts (9:1-19). Paul's experience is nothing short of miraculous. A scrupulous follower of Jewish law, vested with the power to arrest the followers of Jesus, Paul has a mystical experience on the road to Damascus. He encounters the risen Christ as a living reality, confronting him with a new vision of himself and his personal mission. From Paul's perspective, this is not merely a subjective, but results from an encounter with a reality beyond himself, the crucified and risen Christ.

Paul's experience is part a larger story of movement-transforming revelation. Ananias has a similar encounter with the risen Christ in which he is told to welcome the persecutor as God's chosen messenger to the Gentiles. While we can't fully describe the content of either man's experience, it is clear that both of them had visionary experiences that enlightened their minds, warmed their hearts, and gave direction to their lives. Both men are chosen to play a role in the working out of God's vision for human life: Ananias as a mentor; Paul as an evangelist and proclaimer of Jesus' message to the Gentile world.

We often forget the importance of Ananias. What would have happened if Ananias had rejected the message he received as a result of his fear of Paul's (then known as "Saul") reputation as a persecutor? What was it about Ananias that enabled him to receive God's message in the first place? Revelation isn't random. It comes often as a surprise, but it always reflects God's intentions for persons in particular and humankind in general.

Based on this life-changing experience, Paul can claim that "the gospel proclaimed by me is not of human origin, for I did not receive it from a human source ... but through a revelation of Jesus' Christ" (1:12). No doubt Paul studied with wise disciples such as Ananias, learning the stories of Jesus' ministry, death, and resurrection. It is the living Christ, however, that gives Paul confidence that his message is true. The former persecutor is now willing to risk his life to share the good news of Jesus as Christ, the Messiah, who embodies and fulfills God's vision of Shalom, God's realm in human life.

The Meaning Of Revelation (1:13-17)

Throughout Galatians, Paul claims that his authority is directly from God and not from human sources. His encounter with the risen Christ is the source of a new identity, perspective, and vocation. Still, as life-changing as Paul's encounter was, it is clear that his revelatory experience is intimately related to his personal autobiography as a zealous follower of the Jewish religious tradition. Paul's unique perspective challenges us to reflect on the nature of revelation. What would your initial response be if someone proclaimed, "God spoke to me" or "God told me to share this truth with you"? Most of us who are Christians believe that God is still speaking to humankind and addresses in personal ways. We also believe that revelation must be tested and, despite a person's ardor and belief that God has spoken to her or him, we must look at both the source and content of the message. Paul's initial listeners were amazed, perplexed, apprehensive, and suspicious. They needed to be convinced that Paul was truly a transformed person and that his message was congruent with the teachings of Jesus and the first apostles.

As theologian H. Richard Niebuhr asserted, the Holy One who is a reality beyond us is always experienced *within* the relativities of culture, historical, and individual biography. Revelation requires a receiver and is always contextual.[10] Paul's encounter with Christ is

---

10 H. Richard Niebuhr, *The Meaning of Revelation* (New York: Macmillan, 1960).

real. His encounter is also personal and shaped by his own history as an ardent follower of the Jewish tradition. As such, Paul's experience on the Damascus Road and his message reflect a particular historical, religious, and personal perspective. We can imagine that Jesus' other followers, including James of Jerusalem, representing the traditionalist movement; Peter, reflecting the moderate movement; and the teachers who directly criticized Paul's orthodoxy, also had spiritual experiences that shaped their messages. Perhaps, they believed in the truth of their positions with the same passion as Paul proclaimed his gospel spiritual and cultural liberation.

The biblical tradition asserts that only God is absolute. Mystical experiences and direct encounters with the Holy are always shaped by our personal and communal experience. As the theologian Paul Tillich notes, we can hold in contrast our certainty about our experiences of God with the limitations of our particular perspective and expressions of faith.[11] The apostle Paul recognizes the limits of revelation and the varieties of Christian experience when he states, "neither circumcision or uncircumcision is anything; but a new creation is everything" (Galatians 6:15).

How we understand revelation shapes our understanding of scripture and attitudes toward other Christians and persons of other faith traditions. Can there be more than one perspective on the truth? Can we learn important truths and practices from persons of other faiths? Does God speak in many voices, and not just one? Sadly, we have witnessed what happens when people uncritically claim to know God's will and then put it in practice in the public sphere. History is littered by the wreckage created by inquisitions, crusades, holy wars, and jihads.

Grace, Vocation, and Transformation (1:11-17)

Paul sees divine providence at work in his Damascus Road experience and throughout his life. Paul claims "God who set me apart before I was born and called me through his grace, was pleased

---

11 Paul Tillich, *The Dynamics of Faith* (New York: Harper and Brothers), 1958.

to reveal his Son to me, so that I might proclaim him among the Gentiles" (Galatians 1:15-16). Paul believes that his family of origin and his zeal for his faith were not accidental, but reflect divine wisdom every step of the way.

Paul's words echo the prophet Jeremiah's experience of divine providence: "Before I formed you in the womb, I knew you and before you were born, I consecrated you; I appointed you a prophet to the nations" (Jeremiah 1:5). God is at work in every life as the source of insight, inspiration, and synchronous encounters. While few of us have dramatic Damascus Road experiences, God calls forth our gifts, talents, and vocations. Each of us has a place within the body of Christ. Our gifts support the well-being of the whole and are connected with the gifts and talents of everyone within the community.

Paul's description of God's providential movements in his life challenges us to discover and develop our own vocations. Where are you experiencing God's call in your life? Where are you encountering God's Spirit moving in your life in "sighs too deep for words?" Could otherwise random events and encounters be invitations to deepen your understanding of God's calling in your life? While I don't believe that God predestines or acts unilaterally in particular moments of creative transformation and vocational consciousness, I do believe that God calls them forth and invites us to God's companions in sharing good news in our world.

Sources of Authority (1:18-24)

Paul asserts that his message, authority, and vocation come directly from God without help from any human source (1:12). He also claims to have spent time in conversation with James the brother of Jesus and Peter three years after his Damascus Road experience (1:18-19). Fourteen years later, inspired by a revelation, Paul returned to Jerusalem to share his understanding with the leaders of the church "to make sure that I was not running or had not run, in vain" (2:2). Although Paul claims equality with Peter and James, he also recognizes that his authority depends on the congruence of his message with the other apostles' messages and the affirmation of Jesus' earliest followers. In spite of what Paul says, we are compelled to ask the following questions: Did Paul profit in terms of his understanding of Jesus and his message from his experiences with Jesus' first disciples? Did their accounts of Jesus' ministry enrich Paul's understanding of the gospel? Although Paul's letters focus on Christ's liberating work rather than the details of Christ's ministry, no doubt Paul spent much time listening to stories about Jesus' radical hospitality. His embrace of Gentiles as equals may have been inspired by Jesus' all-embracing healing ministry and table fellowship.

Nearly two thousand years later theologian Albert Outler coined the term "Wesleyan Quadrilateral" as a helpful method for discerning theological and doctrinal truth. Following the insights of John Wesley, the parent of the Methodist tradition, Outler believed that healthy theology emerges from the dynamic interplay of scripture, tradition, reason, and experience, to which I would add the highest achievements of culture and science.

Bumper sticker theology such as "the Bible says it, I believe it, and that settles it" is insufficient for a vital and relevant faith. Scriptural insights need to be balanced by the wisdom of the church throughout history, our experiences of God's presence in our lives, philosophical and literary insights, and scientific and medical theories. An omnipresent and loving God "within whom we live and move and have our being" (Acts 17:28) moves through every aspect of our lives, even those typically identified as secular. God is present in the laboratory and medical theatre as well as the theological library, pulpit, and pastor's study. Mystical experiences and revelations from God need to be examined in light of divine wisdom present in the ongoing traditions of the church, understandings of scripture, and ethical reflection. In the spirit of Puritan pastor John Robinson, "God has more light to break forth from his holy word."

Questions for Discussion

1) Take time to read Acts 9:1-19. What do you think of Paul's experience of the risen Christ? What do you think of Ananias' experience of Christ? Do you think people can have direct encounters with God? What do you think of both of them receiving a similar revelation virtually simultaneously?

2) Have you ever encountered someone who said "God spoke to me?" What was your response?

3) Nearly half of all North Americans claim to have had transcendent or spiritual experiences. Have you ever had a mystical experience of God? How did it change your life?

4) Why is it important for Paul to affirm his Jewish credentials? How does this bolster his case against his orthodox critics?

5) What role does human experience have in shaping our encounters with God? Can we experience God apart from the impact of culture, ethnicity, or religion?

6) How does Paul understand the content of his mystical encounter with Christ? What does Christ say to him?

7) Why is it important for Paul to claim over and over that he did not consult with the Jerusalem leaders or any other authority figures (1:12, 17)? Would having learned about Christ from others undercut Paul's message?

8) Using your imagination, what do you think Paul was doing when he went up to Arabia? In these "lost years," whom might Paul have encountered? What might he have learned from other followers of Jesus (1:17)?

9) What is Paul's understanding of providence? Are we really chosen before we are born? Do we have any agency in responding to God's call? How would you describe the relationship between God's will and human decision-making and actions (1:15-16)?

10) Do you think we need to test revelatory experiences by other criteria such as reason, tradition, the wisdom of the community, and scripture? How do these serve as safeguards as well as supports to revelatory experiences?

Closing Prayer

Awaken us, O God, to the rhythms of your Holy Spirit in our lives that all of our days might be sacred and every encounter holy. In Christ's name. Amen.

UNITY AND DIVERSITY

GALATIANS 2:1-14

Vision

Participants will continue to reflect on Paul's understanding of spiritual authority, especially his own authority in the church, his attitudes toward the recognized religious leaders, Peter and James, and the emerging tensions in the early Christian movement. While there is no clear scholarly consensus that Paul's description of his meetings in Jerusalem relate to the account of Jerusalem Council found in Acts 15: 1-35, the similarities are close enough that careful reading of Acts 15 places Paul's comments in Galatians 2:1-14 in a wider historical and theological context.

Prayer

Take time for stillness and then ask the congregants to share the names of Christian communities (denominations) that differ from their own in theology, governance, ethnicity, and worship style. As a group, pray together: *God of many peoples, worshiped in many ways, help us to appreciate the diverse ways people worship and serve you. Let us affirm our kinship with our Christian sisters and brothers and find common cause with them as your companions in healing the world.*

The Jerusalem Council (2:1-10)

Paul's Letter to the Galatians raises the question: Can Christians radically disagree with one another without calling each other names or defining the other's position as a heresy or non-Christian? Paul is severe in his cursing of his opponents. Did his passionate anger serve as a rationale for future denunciations and persecutions within the Christian community?

Over the centuries, Christians have excommunicated each other, burned their opponents at the stake, and censored one another as a result of differing theological viewpoints. One need not go far to remember the controversy between Augustine and Pelagius over humankind's role in relationship to God's grace. Are we passive recipients of grace (Augustine) or can we open ourselves to a greater influx of grace, and cooperate with grace, by spiritual practices and ethical integrity (Pelagius)? This same theological controversy was played out centuries later when strict Calvinists, believing in the predestination of the saved and damned alike, defined Arminius and later John Wesley as heretics, for affirming that humans have the choice whether or not to accept God's grace. The great scientist-priest Teilhard de Chardin was silenced by the Roman Catholic Church in the 1950's for his views on evolution, now fully accepted by Roman Catholic theology. Gay and lesbian persons have been taken off church roles, demonized, and blamed for hurricanes, tornados, and the terrorist attacks on 9/11. Virtually everyone has one ancestor who was defined as a heretic or excommunicated as a result of their beliefs or practices! The schismatic nature of doctrinal and ecclesiastical absolutism has inspired many Christians to take a non-creedal approach to most matters of faith, motivated by the recognition that creeds have as often led to exclusion rather than unity in the church.

Finally, the Letter to the Galatians also raises the question: How important is cultural diversity in expressing our faith? Can we affirm the centrality of Christ and allow Christ's saving power to be expressed in my voices and practices of many cultures?

The occasion of the Jerusalem Council and Paul's Letter to the Galatians is similar. Acts of the Apostles identifies the conservative-traditionalist group as "certain individuals from Judea" who proclaimed that "Unless you are circumcised according to the custom of Moses, you cannot be saved" (Acts 15:1). This created a schism between Paul's free-spirited position and the Jewish-Christian traditionalist position, described as "no small dissension and debate" (Acts 15:2). The Antioch congregation appointed Paul and Barnabas to go to Jerusalem to present the case for a Gentile affirming, non-kosher Christianity. Despite the influence of the conservative movement, the Jerusalem Council sided with Paul's position and sought to find a middle path between Paul's liberalism and the more conservative traditionalists. The Jerusalem leaders affirmed the integrity of ministries to the Gentiles and did not require Gentile males to submit to circumcision. The only requirement was that Gentiles should refrain from "things polluted by idols and fornication and from whatever has been strangled and from blood" (Acts 15:19).

In the Acts account, Peter appears to be the primary public mediator between the warring parties. It is Peter, perhaps fresh from his life-changing vision in Joppa and the descent of the Holy Spirit upon Cornelius (Acts 10), not Paul, who presents the case for an inclusive and egalitarian faith, broad enough to include diverse practices. Peter argues that the coming of God's Spirit affirms that Gentiles as well as Jews are saved by grace and should not be required to give up their culture. Paul, then, steps up to support Peter's viewpoint by sharing the signs and wonders occurring among the Gentile communities. If God's Spirit is alive among the Gentiles, as Peter and Paul assert, then Gentiles should be treated as first-class Christians.

The Jerusalem leaders send a letter, delivered by Paul, to the Christian community in Antioch, Syria, detailing their decision to affirm the integrity of their spiritual experiences (Acts 15:22-35). The Jerusalem decision is met with rejoicing among the mixed Christian communities in Antioch, and presumably among Gentiles throughout the Mediterranean world. The gist of the letter is "you can be free to be yourself and affirm your culture," only observe a few dietary and lifestyle practices that will distinguish you from the society around you.

Paul's account in Galatians 2:1-10 reports a positive response from the Jerusalem leaders. Although the details differ somewhat from the account in Acts 15, Paul's account also describes a group of Christians who oppose the spiritual freedom of the Gentile Christians. In Paul's account in Galatians, the Jerusalem leaders also affirm Paul's authority and understanding of the gospel and entrust him with the ministry to the Gentiles. Peter is given leadership over the ministry to the Jewish communities. In retrospect, Paul's account of the Jerusalem decision raises the following questions: Was the division of responsibilities a wise one? Did it lead to conflicts such as the one between Paul and Peter, described in Galatians 2:11-14? In the pluralistic world of the Roman Empire in which Jewish and Gentile Christians often worshiped beside one another, will the "separate but equal" division of ministries lead to conflicts between traditionalists and liberals, and burdensome requirements for Gentile Christians?

Paul and the Other Leaders (2:1-10)

In Galatians 2, Paul is walking an ecclesiastical and relational tightrope. He makes clear that his message and authority come straight from Jesus Christ, and that he was not tutored by other leaders of the church. He speaks with the authority of Christ and not his own or that of the other leaders. Yet, Paul must also affirm the authority of James, Peter, and others Christian leaders to maintain the unity of the church and his own credibility as a member of the recognized leadership of the emerging movement. To distance himself too far from Jesus' first disciples risks schism in the early Christian movement and the likely disenfranchisement of the new Gentile converts. Paul's theological liberalism and radical hospitality will gain credibility among other, more established Christian communities only if it is clearly connected with the insights and experiences of other Christian leaders.

Counsel to the Gentiles (2:10)

A popular children's album in the 1960's proclaimed, "free to be you and me." In many ways, that's the message the Jerusalem leadership gives to the Gentile Christians in Antioch and Galatia. In the Acts 15 account, the leadership affirms that God's Spirit is at work in their communities and only asks them to refrain from certain dietary practices. They need to make a break from the Temple cults and food sacrificed to idols and adapt a few fairly innocuous aspects of the kosher dietary laws. In his account of the decision of the Jerusalem leadership, Paul omits these dietary requirements and asserts that the only requirement, if this can be called a requirement, is that the Gentiles are to demonstrate their faith through generosity to poor and vulnerable persons.

Paul ultimately sees following the cleanliness or kosher rules of Judaism as spiritually indifferent. What matters is God's new creation, not circumcision or non-circumcision (6:15). In terms of diet, a new Christian may eat whatever he or she desires as long as it isn't a bad influence on impressionable, or "weaker" members of the community. The words of 1 Corinthians 8 reflect Paul's more thought-out reflections on following the Jewish dietary laws, required by the Jerusalem leadership:

> *But food does not bring us near to God; we are no worse if we do not eat, and no better if we do. Be careful, however, that the exercise of your rights does not become a stumbling block to the weak. For if someone with a weak conscience sees you, with all your knowledge, eating in an idol's temple, won't that person be emboldened to eat what is sacrificed to idols? So this weak brother or sister, for whom Christ died, is destroyed by your knowledge. When you sin against them in this way and wound their weak conscience, you sin against Christ. Therefore, if what I eat causes my brother or sister to fall into sin, I will never eat meat again, so that I will not cause them to fall.*   (1 Corinthians 8:8-13)

This practice has been important in my own Christian leadership. As a pastor of a village church whose membership includes many recovering and struggling alcoholics, I choose never to order wine at a restaurant or serve alcohol in my home if I know an alcoholic is present. While I recognize that I am not responsible for other peoples' decisions, I believe that we need to recognize that our behavior influences others for good or ill. This is what it means to be part of the body of Christ.

Trouble In Antioch: Separate But Equal? (2:11-14)

Paul's confidence in the Jerusalem leadership's good faith is short-lived. He is no doubt delighted at Peter's affirmation of the Gentiles. Peter appears to have become part of the non-kosher party until some emissaries of James arrive. Paul's account suggests that they make trouble for Peter, criticizing him for his willingness cross ethnic boundaries and share meals, and perhaps a non-kosher diet, with the Gentile Christians. Peter withdraws from the Gentile community and chooses to eat solely with Jews following the kosher or cleanliness dietary code.

To Paul this is an act of treason against the good news of Jesus Christ, who breaks down every barrier of race, ethnicity, gender, economics, and sexuality. The importance of Peter's withdrawal cannot be overestimated, since it was common for the communal meal to involve the celebration of the Lord's Supper. If Gentiles and Jews can't eat together, they can't jointly celebrate the Eucharist.

Peter's withdrawal defines the Gentiles as second-class Christians, inherently inferior to their so-called Jewish brothers and sisters. There is something wrong with them which can only be remedied by male circumcision and a kosher diet. As United States' history clearly portrays, "separate but equal" is inherently unequal. No wonder Paul, like the civil rights protesters of the 1950s and 1960s, is vehement about maintaining the spiritual equality of the Gentile Christian communities. Paul is so upset at Peter's withdrawal that he publicly calls him out, accusing him of a failure of nerve, bounding on hypocrisy.

At this point, a brief comment on the inherent challenges regarding diet and lifestyle related to Antioch, Syria, is in order. In the first century, Antioch was the third largest city in the Roman Empire. Scholars believe that it had a large Jewish population, some of which were attracted to the message of salvation, obtained through the life, death, and resurrection of the messiah and rabbi Jesus. Most likely Jewish converts to the Christian movement mixed freely with the majority Gentile population as an economic and civil necessity. Further, this same melting pot – or spiritual stew – was likely characteristic of the Christian congregations in the Mediterranean world. While the Jerusalem Council asserted that God's grace embraced both Jews and Gentiles, the recorded evidence in both Galatians and Acts of the Apostles suggests that the Council had not fully clarified ethnic relationships within the church. This lack of clarity likely let to the conflict between Paul and Peter.

We will never know Peter's ultimate reason for withdrawing from the Gentile Christians. Was he intimidated by the emissaries from Jerusalem? Was he trying to keep the peace? Or was he trying to follow a middle-of-the-road position, hoping that as time passed the Gentiles would be accepted as spiritual equals, united in Christ? I would love to hear Peter's account of his encounter with Paul or an explanation of his change of behavior, but it is clear that Peter's moderate viewpoint pleases no one, either the conservative traditionalists or the radical liberal Paul. Paul is unwilling to compromise, and his response resembles Martin Luther King's response to white moderates in "Why We Can't Wait." Christ's cross means freedom now, and God's dream of graceful unity can't be deferred by ethnic superiority or tradition. We will never know if Peter changed his mind, but for Paul this was one more reason to respond directly to any attempt to compel Gentiles to adopt Jewish practices to become full followers of Jesus Christ.

Questions for Discussion

1) After reading Paul's and Acts of the Apostles' accounts of the meeting in Jerusalem (Acts 15:1-34; Galatians 2:1-10), consider the following questions: How are the accounts similar to one another? How do they differ? Do you think they definitively solved the problems related to the emerging Gentile churches? How might they have decided differently to avoid the conflict of Peter and Paul in Antioch and the attempts to convert Gentile Christians to kosher Christianity in Galatia?

2) Paul once more speaks of acting as a result of a revelation (2:2). He is not specific about the nature of this divine guidance. How do you think God revealed God's directions to Paul? Does God still speak to people today? In what ways does God speak to people? Have you experienced divine guidance, or revelation, in your life?

3) Paul has an ambivalent attitude toward other religious leaders (2:6). In what ways is Paul's attitude reflective of his understanding of his spiritual authority and the nature of God's revelation to him? How does his language differentiate himself from the other leaders of the church? How does his language affirm their leadership?

4) What was Paul's reason initially for going to the Jerusalem church? What are the results of the visit with the other leaders? What is asked of Paul in his missionary work and the Gentile communities (2:7-10)?

5) Paul speaks of the Jerusalem leaders affirming the "grace that had been given to me" (2:9). What do you think this "grace" was? What is the nature of grace described in this passage and throughout Galatians?

6) Who are these people who are spying on the freedom of Paul's Galatian community? What is the nature of this Gentile freedom as far as you can ascertain (2:3-5)?

7) Have you ever had the experience of refraining from certain otherwise innocuous behaviors because they would be a bad influence on others or might lead others astray?

8) In Antioch, Paul confronts Peter about his apparent hypocrisy. What is the problem Peter creates, according to Paul? Looking at the issue from Peter's standpoint, why does he withdraw from the Gentiles? What do you think about the author's notion that Peter is attempting a middle ground position? Do you think Peter's middle ground approach is helpful?

Closing Prayer

Holy One, we confess the tragic impact of ethnic, sexual, economic, theological, and racial separation in the church. Help us to live out your radical hospitality, honoring your diverse body, while maintaining the spirit of our own traditions. Let our communion meals be open to all who seek to follow you and let us welcome your many faces in church and in the world. In Christ's name. Amen.

Lesson Four

The Dynamics of Grace

Galatians 2:15-3:18

Vision

Grace is central to the Apostle Paul's understanding of our relationship with God. In this lesson, participants will ponder Paul's understanding of the relationship of grace and law, and see grace as trust in and openness to God's love for us, regardless of our situation. Participants will reflect on Abraham as a "knight of faith" (Soren Kierkegaard) for whom God's initiative is an invitation to agency and adventure. God's grace to Abraham is global, going beyond the confines of Jewish law, to embrace all people.

Participants will experience Abraham as a mediator of grace, first to all humanity, and later to the Jewish people. Accordingly, the circle of grace is wider than the boundaries of law. God's covenant with the Gentiles, given to Abraham several hundred years before the Mosaic law, places Jews and Gentiles on equal footing as sinners in need of grace.

Prayer

Let us begin our time with silence, breathing in God's energy of love.

Loving God, your grace is sufficient for us. Help us to trust you with our lives, recognizing that your grace frees us from the past and awakens us to a wide open future. Help us to lean not on our own individual achievements, and even our own goodness, but trust your grace, and the synergy of your grace and our response in taking our role as your beloved companions in sharing grace to others. In Jesus' name. Amen.

Grace, Faith, And Righteousness (2:15-21)

At the heart of Paul's challenge to his fellow Christian teachers is their understanding of grace. They appear to believe that grace only comes into effect when we observe the ancient laws of Judaism. Paul believes that he knows better. He had been an ardent follower of law prior to his encounter with Jesus on the road to Damascus. His encounter with the Risen One challenged his previous law-based existence and invited him to share in the freedom of God's graceful spirit. Paul had much to repent. There was Christian blood on his hands. But even his antagonism to the early Christian movement was overcome and then transformed by the grace of the crucified and risen Christ. As Paul was to affirm in Romans, "God proves God's love for us in that while we were still sinners Christ died for us" (Romans 5:8). Moreover, just as sin and death, Paul believed, entered the world, shaping every human life, through Adam's turning from God, so too Jesus' "act of righteousness of righteousness leads to justification and life for all" (Romans 5:18). Grace is universal, unmerited, and given to us in spite of our turning for God's path for our lives. Grace reminds us that even when we run away from God, we will eventually run into God's loving arms.

Three key words are present in Galatians – grace, justification, and faith. Put simply, grace is God's love embodied in the life, death, and resurrection of Jesus Christ. The cross of Christ is victorious over sin and liberates us to live freely through God's Spirit. Grace can't be earned, but is God's loving gift for all who have gone astray. Earning God's love by following the law ends up separating us from the grace of God. God gives us everything, but we want to justify ourselves as if the cross and resurrection never occurred. We can't nullify God's grace by our dependence on Jewish law; but we can diminish our experience of grace.

Jesus' ministry was embodied grace. He reached out to sinners, foreigners, and outcasts, inviting them into God's realm just as they were in all their brokenness and alienation. Jesus sacrificed for those who turned away from him. On the cross, Jesus shared grace with his persecutors, interceding with God, saying, "Father, forgive them; they do not know what they are doing" (Luke 23:34).

Faith is our opening to God's freely given grace. God calls and we respond, and when we say "yes" to grace, miracles happen. A woman who had been bleeding comes to Jesus, and touches him, whispering to herself, "If I but touch his clothes, I will be made well" (Mark 5:28). Healing power is released and she is cured, body, mind, and spirit. She is restored to society after years of alienation. Jesus pronounces, "Daughter, your faith has made you well; go in peace, and be healed of your disease" (Mark 5:34). Jesus invites Levi, a hated tax collector, to follow him, and when Levi follows, his life is forever transformed.

Faith is not a "work," an action that we perform or a belief we hold, to earn God's love. Faith is opening our lives to God's love and letting God guide us into an adventurous future. When Paul speaks of being "justified by faith in Christ, and not by doing the works of law" (2:16), he is affirming that our faith reconciles us with God, overcomes our sin, and enables us to become a new creation. God has already acted to overcome the alienation between humanity and God; justification has already occurred from God's side, and we have been made right with God by God's initiative, and now we know it! In light of God's grace, which overcomes every human barrier, we can say, with the late Ernie Campbell, preaching professor and pastor of Riverside Church in New York, "there are only two kinds of people in the world: those who are in God's hands and know it, and those who are in God's hands and don't." The interplay of grace, faith, and justification awaken us to our standing as God's beloved, regardless of the past or any human condition, and liberate us to God's glorious new creation in our hearts and in the world.

Those Galatian Sinners!

Paul makes an apparently insulting comment regarding his Gentile followers, regarding their status as sinners. Paul's remark suggests that he has two audiences in mind: Gentile Christians being swayed by the traditionalist Christian movement and moderate Jewish Christians whom Paul may win over to his position, thus tipping the balance toward his inclusive vision of the Gospel.

I believe that Paul's use of "sinners" to describe Gentiles relates to a sociological or religious, rather than moral, category. In the Gospels, certain people – persons with illnesses, foreigners, and certain occupations, such as tax collectors – are referred to as sinners based on their outsider status. Their social or health status rendered them unable to enter the temple or synagogue and relate to the righteous ones. Sinfulness refers then to uncleanliness rather than immorality.[12]

Paul's Gentile listeners may have been aware of this distinction, invoked in Paul's presentation of the good news of Jesus, which bridged the categories of clean and unclean. In contrast, Paul's conservative opponents might have reminded the Gentiles that, despite the saving work of Jesus, they were unclean until they adopted Jewish dietary and ritualistic practices.

Grace and Law (3:1-14)

Like many of her generation, my mother returned to the work force in midlife when my brother and I were teenagers. Her first interview after receiving her early childhood education credential was for a teaching position at a local Christian school. She was shocked by the first question from the principal: "You know we are a Christian school. We need to know if you wear makeup, dance, or go to movies. These are all forbidden for our faculty." Recently, a new member of our church noted that she left organized religion when her pastor refused to baptize her grandchild because

---

12 Greg Carey, *Sinners: Jesus and His Earliest Followers* (Waco: Baylor University Press, 2009).

the parents weren't married. In more recent times, a number of denominations have refused ordination for persons as a result of their gender – after all, they claim that the Bible says women can't be ministers or instruct men on spiritual issues – or sexual identity, gay and lesbians by their behavior have forfeited God's love. These stories all beg the questions, "What is essential in Christian faith? What is the relationship between God's grace and our community's particular rules and mores?"

For Paul, the freedom that comes from God's grace is everything. Christ has set us free to be his followers in the world. Accordingly, we don't need to be imprisoned by the absolute edicts of the religion police. Paul was shocked when he was confronted with the legalism demanded by fellow Christians in Galatia. Paul appreciated the value of the Jewish law. Yet, he challenged any form of legalism that made obedience to the letter of the law more important than accepting God's freely given grace. As I noted earlier, he also believed that Christian legalism denied Gentiles equality in the Christian community, thus rupturing the unity we have in Christ, graphically revealed in the celebration of the Lord's Supper. Theologically speaking, making the Jewish law necessary to Christian faith renders the cross of Christ unnecessary.

Theologian Paul Tillich spoke of three approaches to law – autonomy, heteronomy, and theonomy. Autonomy involves being a law unto yourself and following your own ethical path without consideration of the community's well-being or God's vision of our lives. Autonomous approaches to law are reflected in libertarian understandings of citizenship, which assume that the individual is free to do whatever he or she wants in terms of property rights without regards to the well-being the community. They are also reflected in the political sphere when people speak of rights to gun ownership or a woman's right to choose an abortion as absolute, thus denying any responsibility to consider the safety or rights of others. In the first century, certain Christians believed that because of God's grace they could do anything they wanted without consequence. Grace abounds, as Paul will say to the Galatians, but "do not use your freedom for self-indulgence, but through love become slaves to one another" (5:13).

Heteronomy involves external rules imposed "for our own good" or "because I said so." Imposed and often arbitrary laws often alienate children from parents and citizens from their leaders. The demands made by Paul's opponents in Galatia involved requiring Gentiles to adopt religious practices that were foreign to their culture simply because they were in the Jewish law.

In contrast to rule by oneself or others, Paul advocates a form of theonomy, that is, alignment with God's vision for our lives. If God's grace, mediated through the sacrificial love of Christ and manifest in the movements of the Holy Spirit in our lives, is central to Christian faith, then when we live by the Spirit we are also embodying what is essentially best for us. We are following the deeper laws of our own lives, body, mind, and spirit. Put in ordinary everyday terms, certain behaviors, smoking, gluttony, excessive use of alcohol, are to be avoided, not because they are evil, according to others' standards, but because indulging in them destroys our personal well-being and may harm others, physically or spiritually. In a similar fashion, the Hebraic prophets challenge unjust business practices and the accumulation of wealth, while others are homeless and starving, not only because income inequality and unrestrained acquisition of wealth destroys the social fabric and causes pain to God, but because it destroys the spiritual lives of those who perpetuate injustice and poverty by their behaviors. They will, as the prophet Amos proclaims, experience a famine of hearing the world of God, because they have failed to hear the cries of the poor (Amos 8:11).

Theonomous living is based on the congruence between our will and God's vision in which, inspired by the Holy Spirit, we can affirm with Jesus "not my will but thine be done," thus embodying God's realm "on earth as it is in heaven" (Matthew 6:10). In Galatians, Paul will identify theonomous living with the "works of the Spirit." We make sacrifices and limit our freedom because of our love for God and one another, not as a result of fear of punishment or obedience to an external rule.

Christ as the Center (2:19-20)

"I have been crucified with Christ; and it is no longer I who live but Christ who lives in me" (2:20). For Paul, Christian experience is shaped by the cross and resurrection of Jesus. The burden of perfection has been crucified, and now we can live gracefully and boldly, trusting God's grace to transform our imperfect lives into reflections of divine love and beauty.

Following external rules, even the rules of our faith tradition, to earn our relationship with God eventually leads to the burden of failure and guilt. The demands of the law set a standard that is beyond our abilities to meet and the more we try to live up to the law, the more entangled we become in conflicts of our own creation. Living by the law demands obedience and a willing heart. Yet often we obey simply out of duty or obligation, rather than the desire to be aligned with what is best for us and others. Moreover, the impossible demands of perfectly following the law create the conflicts between our inner lives and external behaviors that Paul describes in Romans 7:

> *I do not understand my own actions. For I do not do what I want, but I do the very thing I hate.... For I do not do the good I want, but the evil I do not want is what I do. Now if I do what I do not want, it is no longer I that do it, but sin that dwells within me. For I delight in the law of God in my inmost self, but I see in my members another law at war with the law of my mind, making me captive to the law of sin that dwells in my members. Wretched man that I am! Who will rescue me from this body of death? Thanks be to God through Jesus Christ our Lord!*
>   (Romans 7:15, 19-20, 22-25)

Trusting Christ liberates us from the impossible burdens of the law. In embracing the cross, we experience Christ's death and are reborn as a new creation. The dissonance between God's will and our own is overcome by Christ's new life within us. Now, every-thing centers on Christ. Christ is our inspiration, guide, and inner light. Freed from fear, we experience "Christ in [us], the hope of glory" (Colossians 1:27).

Living by the Spirit (3:1-5)

The Holy Spirit is at the heart of the Galatians' experience of God's grace. God's Spirit, according to Paul, is both universal and personal. It is the Spirit of Pentecost, manifest in wind, fire, and ecstatic speech. It is also the enlivening energy of creation. On the one hand, God's Spirit works through individuals, transform-ing and working miracles in our lives (Galatians 3:1-5, Romans 8:1-17). On the other hand, God's Spirit murmurs in all creation (Romans 8:18-23) and intercedes gently in our own lives in "sighs too deep for words" (Romans 8:26). Moreover God's Spirit enables us to communicate with God ecstatically, as we cry, "Abba, Father" (Galatians 4:6; Romans 8:15).

Although the Spirit dwells in our hearts (Galatians 4:6; Ro-mans 8:11), Paul is clear that the reality of God's Spirit can't be reduced to subjective inner experiences. The Spirit we experience is sent by God, enlivening and enlightening us and giving us new life. God's spirit is within us, yet beyond our own fabrication as a manifestation of God's presence in all creation. The Spirit connects our subjective spiritual experiences with the reality of Christ's death and resurrection and presence in our world today.

Abrahamic Faith (3:15-18)

Like his opponents, Paul sees Abraham as central to God's covenant with humanity. Paul believes that God's key promise to Abraham is centered on the affirmation that "in you all the fami-lies of the earth shall be blessed" (Genesis 12:3). Paul's Christian opponents focus on God's covenant, requiring Jewish males to be circumcised as a sign of the divine-human covenant (Genesis

17:1-14). Take time to read Genesis 12:1-9 and Genesis 17:1-14 to understand the foundational documents Paul and his opponents appeal to as authorities for their position.

Soren Kierkegaard described Abraham – and I would add Sarah – as a knight of faith. Abraham leaves his homeland with nothing but a promise from God. He sacrifices security to be faithful to God's call. He accepts God's promise that a great nation will come from his offspring, despite the fact that he and Sarah are both aged and childless. He is willing to sacrifice Isaac, and the future of his family lineage, in obedience to God. Abraham follows God's call, hoping against hope that he will have a new home, son, and generations of descendants.

This is the heart of faith, according to Paul. We trust God in life and death. We accept God's promises although they run counter to our current life situation. We are willing to depend on God, and not our own achievements, for our future and our salvation. Abraham and Sarah accept grace with no apparent guarantees and, in saying "yes" to God's calling, they become the surprising parents of a great nation and the mediators of God's salvation to the whole earth. Abraham is not merely a Jewish hero. He is the spiritual parent of all people, and a sign that God's grace includes Gentiles, including Muslims who celebrate Abraham's faith, as well as Jews. God's promise to Abraham that all peoples will be blessed through him places Jews and Gentiles on equal footing and makes circumcision optional rather than required in the Gentile – and dare we say, Jewish – communities. In light of God's grace in Christ, prefigured in God's universal covenant with Abraham, Paul can affirm, "neither circumcision nor uncircumciscion is anything; but a new creation is everything" (Galatians 6:15)!

Questions for Discussion

1) What does it mean to be saved by faith? How does Paul understand faith? How do you understand faith (2:15-21)?

2) Does faith require belief in a particular set of doctrines? What might the problem be if we make "orthodoxy" essential to faith?

3) What does Paul mean by "nullifying the grace of God?" Do you agree with him (2:15-21)?

4) What do you think of Paul's use of the word "sinners" to describe Gentiles? What are your thoughts about sin as a relational and sociological, rather than moral, category (2:15)?

5) What does grace mean? Where have you experienced the grace of God? Is it possible to have a strong sense of grace, while deemphasizing sin in Christian preaching and theology (2:15-21)?

6) Paul says "it is not I who live, but Christ who lives in me" (2:20). What do you think this means? What must die to experience God? What does "Christ in me" mean?

7) What is the role of the Spirit in the early Christian community (3:1-5)? Does your church focus on the Holy Spirit, or are Christ or God more often invoked in worship services and other church gatherings?

8) How does Paul contrast "law" and "grace" or "works of law" and "grace of God?" What's the problem with "law"? In what ways does Paul believe it might harm our faith and our relationship with God (3:1-14)?

9) What does it mean to be "justified" by God (3:11)?

10) What is the "promise of Abraham?" How does Paul differentiate between the covenant given to the Gentiles and the one given to the Jewish people (3:15-18)?

Closing Prayer

Holy One, we thank you for the grace that gives us new life. Help us to live by grace and share your grace with others that they too might experience the freedom of knowing they are your beloved children. In Jesus' name. Amen.

LESSON FIVE

OBEDIENCE AND TRANSFORMATION

GALATIANS 3:19-4:7

Vision

After describing the problems of trying to earn our salvation by following the letter of the law, Paul discusses the law as a divine gift to humankind. Participants will explore the positive benefits of the law and its importance in nurturing personal growth and communal well-being. Participants will also consider what it means to be clothed in Christ and reflect on the ramifications of Christian unity for economic, social, and interpersonal relationships.

Prayer

Begin with a time of sharing about the benefits of law in personal and community relationships. Then, silently take time to center through slowly breathing in God's loving presence.

Holy One, we are grateful for your many gifts, including structures of law that encourage order and creativity in our relationships and communities. We rejoice in our unity in Christ and ask that we might see all of your beloved children as clothed in Christ. Help us to bring forth Christ's presence in ourselves and one another. In Jesus' name. Amen.

Law as a Blessing (3:19-24)

Paul appears to be ambivalent about the law's role in our relationship with God and the conduct of human life. On the one hand, no one can ever fully obey the law. All have sinned and fallen short of God's glory and vision for human life (Romans 3:23). We constantly miss the mark in our moral behavior, and often obey the law, whether the laws given by God to Moses and embedded in our being, or civil law, grudgingly. On the other hand, we need the law to maintain civil order, dignity in worship and religious life, and curb our own egocentrism. Paul is not rejecting Judaism or Jewish law. He is just challenging law as the primary foundation for our relationship with God. Paul is clear in Romans that God's covenant with the Jewish people remains in effect even after the coming of Jesus (11:1). If God nullifies God's covenant with Israel, can we rely on God's faithfulness to us? Paul goes so far as to say that in God's vision of salvation, despite the Jewish rejection of Christ, "all Israel will be saved" (11:26). Paul's radical universalism includes creation, the Jew, and the Gentile, for God "may be all in all" (1 Corinthians 15:28).

We can't earn God's love by following the law. In fact, if we see obedience as the primary way of maintaining a positive relationship with God and others, we become alienated from God and our own kinfolk, as Jesus suggests in his description of the older brother in the parable of the Prodigal Son (Luke 15:11-32). But, when we open ourselves to God's unmerited grace, we experience the freedom of God's love and obedience becomes a gift of grace, not an act of will.

Paul is clear that the Jewish law – and I would suspect, just civil laws – are part of God's redemptive purpose. Law exists because of our waywardness and to restrain sin, especially in our personal relations. Law reflects God's promise insofar as it challenges injustice, protects the vulnerable, and maintains social order. Law is a disciplinarian, keeping us in line, like a tutor or nanny, until we can make mature decisions. As a grandparent of two wonderful young boys, I constantly find myself as a source of law and order in my daily interactions with them. Although I try, above all, to give them opportunities for freedom and creativity, I stand at ready to restrain their impulses to run in the street heedless of cars, destroy personal property in the course playing games, or deal with sibling rivalry by hitting each other. I have to remind them about bedtimes and sometimes put them to bed against their will, all for their own good. My relational and behavioral rules are guided by love, not authoritarianism. Paul believes that we are like children, often unaware of the impact of our actions on ourselves and others, until it's too late.

Paul believes that religious law, and in particular, the laws given to the Jewish people, is part of God's gracefulness and is a medium of divine promise. When we realize our inability to fulfill God's law, and experience the realities of guilt and responsibility, we become receptive to a grace beyond our efforts. As Paul says in Romans 7:24-25: "Wretched man that I am! Who will rescue me from this body of death? Thanks be to God through Jesus Christ our Lord!" Law leads us to trusting Christ's death and resurrection, "just as I am, without one plea."

Clothed in Christ (3:25-29)

A Benedictine Monastery in Pennsylvania, where I have often gone on retreat, has a plaque that counsels, "Treat Everyone as Christ." As Matthew 25:31-46 asserts, caring for others is grounded in our commitment to "see everyone as Christ." Paul would be at home with both of these affirmations. In a world in which the "clothes made the man [or woman]" and revealed one's place in the social and economic order to say you are "clothed in Christ" is to affirm that in relationship to God and one another in the church, we are all God's beloved, we are all equals, joined by God's Spirit.

In Christ, we are one. "There is no longer Jew or Greek, there is no longer slave or free, there is no longer male and female" (3:28). Paul's affirmation begs the question: If we are one in Christ, does this unity go beyond the church, dissolving alienation and inequality based on ethnicity, social standing, or gender? Paul's dream of unity goes far beyond the three ethnic, social and economic contrasts he presents in Galatians. Could we take Paul a step further and affirm that in Christ, there is no longer heterosexual or homosexual, white or black, Jew or Palestinian, conservative or liberal? What implications would Paul's vision of unity have on our church governance, ordination requirements, neighborhood policing, Middle East policy, or culture wars? If Christ overcomes every form of alienation, then those who follow Christ must work to do so as well. Does Christ's liberating love take us beyond individual face to face relationships to explore ways to achieve cultural, organizational, and legal reconciliation?

God's Beloved Children (4:1-7)

Paul boldly proclaims that through the life, death, and resurrection of Jesus Christ, we are free from every form of bondage and are welcomed as full heirs and recipients of God's loving parenthood. God is our true parent. Though we have been in a far off land, alienated from God and one another, God has redeemed us and restored us to full membership in God's family. This restoration is reflected in both the external embrace of the body of Christ, animated by God's Spirit, and the internal affirmation of our relationship with God through the presence of the Holy Spirit. God's Spirit testifies to this grace within our spirits, bursting forth with "Abba, Father," and proclaiming God's love in both Aramaic and Greek.

Questions for Discussion

1) What is Paul's understanding of the purpose of the law? Does the law have any positive benefits? What is the negative aspect of law? What aspects of law are troubling to Paul (3:19-27)?

2) In what ways does grace liberate us from the law's power? Do we still need to follow the laws of our community after we have experienced God's Spirit as our defining reality (3:25)?

3) What does it mean to be clothed in Christ? How might this vision change your perspective on life (3:27)?

4) "In Christ there is neither Jew nor Gentile, slave or free, male or female." Why is this important? Do distinctions still remain? Does Paul intend us to be color blind and gender blind? Who else might we welcome as a result of following Paul's affirmation (3:27)?

5) What does it mean to be "one in Christ"? How might this change our behaviors? In what was might this change our economics and politics?

6) What does Paul mean by describing the transformation of persons from slaves to heirs? How would we describe this statement in our time, where issues of slavery are no longer relevant, at least, on the surface[13] (4:1)?

7) How do you understand "the fullness of time" as a description of Jesus' coming to the world (4:5)?

8) What does it mean for us to experience the Spirit saying, "Abba, Father?" Have you ever heard God's inner voice (4:6)?

Concluding Prayer

Abba, Father! Amma, Mother! Help us to experience your Spirit in all things and all things enlivened by your Spirit that we might always walk on holy ground and see holiness in all our companions on this good earth. In Christ's name. Amen.

---

13 We must not forget in our freedom, those who are victims of human trafficking, sweat shops, and sexual slavery.

Spirits Unbound

Galatians 4:8-5:1

Vision

Participants will continue to explore Paul's criticism of Christian legalism. Participants will reflect on their understandings of biblical authority in light of his interpretation of the Sarah-Hagar story. Paul's vision of Christian freedom animates the Letter to the Galatians and his opposition to anything that places this spirit-based freedom in jeopardy.

Prayer

Let us begin by sharing moments when we felt God's presence in a freeing way. How did this freedom change our lives? Then, let us silently give thanks for the freedom we have in God's love through Jesus Christ.

Holy One, you have set us free to love. Your grace has liberated us from the past, the limitations we have placed on ourselves, and the burden of sin. Help us to say "yes" to grace and out of our freedom, let us be channels of graceful liberation to others. In Christ's name. Amen.

Keep Moving Forward (4:8-20)

In Paul's Letter to the Philippians, he describes his own spiritual progress as forward looking with eyes on the prize of salvation.

He affirms, as he does in Galatians, his faithful following of the Jewish Law and his rise in the intellectual elite, and then relativizes his past achievements in light of the grace of God. "Whatever gains I had, I count as loss because of Christ. More than that, I regard everything as loss because of the surpassing value of knowing Jesus Christ my Lord" (Philippians 3:7-8). Alive in Christ, Paul is pressing forward toward the goal of the heavenly call of God in Christ Jesus (3:14). He hasn't yet made it to the goal, but God's horizon of love guides his steps and lures him forward. Faith is about the future, not the past. Embracing Christ's new creation means letting go of anything that stands in the way of our full participation in Christ's life, death, and resurrection.

Paul is perplexed at the Galatians. After experiencing the freedom of God's Spirit, they are falling back into ritualistic and liturgical legalism. In principle, there is nothing wrong with following special days, months, and seasons. I observe the Christian liturgical year, and this morning I was making plans for Advent and Christmas services at the congregation where I serve. The problem is assuming that following the liturgical year, or the seasons of the church, is a requirement and that those who deviate from the liturgical calendar, lectionary readings, or practice topical preaching are second class Christians. As I said earlier, Paul recognizes and affirms cultural and spiritual pluralism. The issue is seeing one pathway as absolute and final, required of all "true" Christians, and all others as inferior or false. The freely moving Spirit of God is not constrained by any texts, church calendars, or ethical absolutes.

Paul's Mysterious Illness (4:12-15)

Paul notes that his initial visit to Galatia was related to a physical infirmity. Could it have been the thorn in the flesh, Paul describes in 2 Corinthians 12:1-6? Was it some illness that Paul contracted on his missionary journeys? There is no clear answer to this question, although some scholars suggest Paul might have been suffering from malaria or a debilitating eye disease. Could Paul's need for convalescence among the Galatian Christians have been necessitated by the after effects of beatings or stoning at the hands of his persecutors? In any event, Paul sees divine providence in his extended stay in Galatia. His illness allowed him to preach the Gospel and form bonds with the Galatian communities. Paul now believes that his intimacy with the Galatians is being threatened by their turning to legalistic approaches to salvation.

A Strange Allegory? (4:21-31)

Paul's allegory of the children of Hagar and Sarah, Ishmael and Isaac, is irrelevant and possibly offensive to many readers. In describing the covenants of law and grace, Paul calls Hagar's son Ishmael the child of a slave and Sarah's child Isaac, the child of a free woman. Stretching the text to the limit, Paul speaks of the slave child persecuting the free child just as legalistic Christians are persecuting Paul. In Paul's allegory, he asserts that the slave child must be driven out and stripped of any the inheritance he may have taken. Moreover, the free child apparently has no moral obligations to his enslaved half-brother.

The accounts found in Genesis, chapters 16, 17 and 21, give a better sense of the relationship of Hagar and Sarah, and Ishmael and Isaac. Although Ishmael, son of Hagar a slave woman, is Abraham's first born, God's covenant is with Sarah's yet unborn child. Childless Sarah initially supports the "surrogate" male child and her mother. However, over time, Sarah becomes jealous. Hagar and Ishmael are sent away, presumably to die in the wilderness, but are rescued by God's providential response to Hagar's pleas. Ishmael takes second place in Abraham's and God's eyes, but he also receives an inheritance and becomes the father of a nation. Today, Muslims see Ishmael as an important prophet, while Judaism and Christianity typically ignore him or downplay his importance. Does this disparity still shape Jewish-Muslim relationships? Further, does Paul's problematic use of the categories of slave and free, and the obvious inferiority of the slave child, support an implicit racism within the Christian faith? Did not God also show divine faithfulness to Hagar and Ishmael, who were abandoned in the wilderness through no fault of their own?

What is clear is that Paul is no biblical literalist. He sees scripture in "post-modern" terms as a living text, shaped as much by the interpreter and reader as the original author. Paul freely uses the Sarah and Hagar stories to assert that covenant of grace which Christians experience comes through Abraham and Isaac rather than the legalism, identified with Hagar and Ishmael. This initial covenant is more extensive, and just as authoritative, as the covenant of circumcision and the later laws of Mount Sinai.

Freedom Takes Commitment (5:1)

After Paul's laborious allegorical journey, he delivers one of the great affirmations of scripture: "For freedom, Christ has set us free. Stand firm therefore and do not submit again to the yoke of slavery" (5:1). Two important concepts emerge from Paul's affirmation. First, Christ is our liberator. Following Jesus opens a new world of possibility to us. God's goal is to nurture freedom and creativity. God wants us to freely accept grace and then utilize our freedom to heal the world. God does not want to keep us enslaved. God's desire is that we be agents of our own destiny in line with the Holy Spirit's movements in our lives. Faithfulness means freedom, innovation, novelty, and growth.

Paul recognizes, based on his experience with the Galatians, that freedom requires spiritual vigilance. It is tempting to fall back into legalism and passivity. Like the children of Israel, we may, when the going gets rough, desire to return to the predictable bondage of Egypt rather than the creative insecurity of God's liberating love. Christian freedom requires constantly choosing to follow the path of the Spirit, guided by love and open to improvisation.

Questions for Discussion

1) What does Paul mean by enslavement to elemental spirits? Do we see people imprisoned in their spiritual lives or by forces beyond themselves (4:8-11)?

2) Are there positive benefits to observing certain rituals and seasons, special days and years? Why might legalistic understandings of ritual be problematic (4:10)?

3) Using your imagination, what is your understanding of Paul's physical infirmity? Has an illness ever served to advance your spiritual life or sense of vocation (4:13)?

4) What does it mean for Paul to affirm that Christ is being formed in the Galatian Christians? How does this formation occur and what supports our spiritual formation (4:19)? In what ways or by what practices might Christ be formed more fully in us?

5) What do you make of Paul's use of the relationship of Sarah and Hagar? Does it make any sense today? How do you feel about his identification of Hagar's child as being born for slavery (4:21-31)?

6) How do you understand biblical authority? Are the words of scripture final and unchanging? Or, do they provide a basis for many possible interpretations and theological positions, as Paul appears to assume in Galatians 4:21-31?

7) "For freedom Christ has set us free. Stand firm, therefore, and do not submit again to a yoke of slavery" (5:1). What do you think that passage means? What is our freedom? In contrast, what enslaves us today? Are our temptations to return to the yoke of slavery similar to or different from the Galatians?

Closing Prayer

Free Spirit of God, open us to the freedom of new creation, liberate us from sin and past achievements, that we may follow you anew today as your creative companions in shaping a just and graceful world. In Jesus' name. Amen.

THE WORKS OF THE SPIRIT

GALATIANS 5:2-26

Vision

Participants will reflect on Paul's understanding of the Holy Spirit as the inner source of Christian freedom and consider Paul's relativizing of rituals and theologies in light of God's new creation. Further, participants will contrast the works of flesh and spirit and explore their social, economic, and relational implications.

Prayer

God's Holy Spirit is often identified with breath (pneuma). In a time of silence, breathe deeply and with each breath open to God's Spirit with the words "I breathe the Spirit deeply in." Exhale any stresses or burdens into God's loving care.

Loving God, let your Spirit be born in our hearts. May we reflect your Spirit in all that we do, as we experience the freedom of God's new creation animating our lives. In Christ's name. Amen.

What Is It About Grace That You Don't Understand? (5:2-6)

Paul's manifesto for Christian freedom is about creativity and relationship, not passivity and independence. Our quest to justify ourselves on our own, and through our ability to follow the law, breaks the connection between God and ourselves. It basically says to God, "I don't need you. The cross doesn't matter. I can do it myself." But, just like my young children, who sometimes want to be independent and do some task by themselves, their apparent independence actually depends on an infrastructure of grace and support, most particularly, our love, home, and vigilance.

Moreover, if we seek to justify ourselves by our quest for perfection, we eventually find ourselves judging others to see if they are further along spiritually than we are. We also will bolster our own egos by noting how much further along we are than those who fail to keep the law, whether as a result of ethnicity, for example, the uncircumcised Gentile males, or moral lapses and intentional wrong doing. We will be grateful that we are not like all those other people, who just don't get God's message – for example, depending on our perspective, Democrats, Republicans, fundamentalists, liberals, substance abusers, unfaithful spouses, and parents of "problem children." For Paul, the cross and the law, ironically, challenge self-made morality and independence, as they reveal to us our need for God and a loving community to find wholeness in our lives.

Everything is grace, Paul proclaims. Our ability to express our freedom creatively depends on God's graceful order in the universe, sunrise and sunset, seed time and harvest, and God's continuous providence in our lives. This is the grace of interdependence, most fully revealed in Paul's image of the body of Christ (1 Corinthians 12:12-31), in which each part's ability to express its gifts and vocation depends on all the other parts and the well-being of the whole depends on the positive contribution of each part.

Grace relativizes all our rituals, doctrines, and practices. God's grace may even relativize Paul's own antagonism to the kosher and circumcision party of the Christian movement. As Paul notes in a moment of gentle self-transcendence, "For in Christ Jesus neither circumcision nor uncircumcision counts for anything; the only thing that counts is faith working through love" (5:6).

To the Jewish conservatives, Paul chides, "Remember what's really important. Is it the rule book or God's love for us? God doesn't need circumcision and dietary practices to heal our spirits." To the Gentile community, Paul counsels, "Don't worry about circumcision. If deep down circumcision feels right as a response to God's freely given grace, go ahead. If a particular diet helps you deepen your spiritual life and become a good influence on others, go ahead. But, remember, these rituals are responses to God, not ways to earn God's love. If you don't feel a necessity for circumcision, that's fine, too. It's not necessary for your relationship with God. God loved you before you knew Christ and God loves you regardless of your diet or ritual practices."

Paul's contrast between what's essential – "faith working through love" – and what's optional invites us to ask ourselves and our communities: What practices in our church have we made "sacred cows?" What beliefs or rituals do we use to show our superiority to others? What practices unnecessarily separate us from our Christian – and non-Christian – brothers and sisters? One doesn't need to go far to remember conflicts over adult and infant baptism, baptism by immersion or sprinkling, wine or grape juice for communion, not to mention the ordination of women, persons who have been divorced, or the full acceptance of gay and lesbian persons. My own denomination, the Christian Church (Disciples of Christ), split with what is today called the Christian Church over whether the Bible affirmed or prohibited the use of organs and pianos in worship. Regardless of how our churches respond to diversity of practice and belief, we need to remember that God's love poured into our hearts is the one absolute, and not our traditions and practices, within the body of Christ. Paul knows, first hand, as he looks back on his own spiritual journey, that our well-intentioned and spiritually-justifiable attempts at orthodoxy can lead us away from God's vision for our lives.

Called to Freedom (5:7-15)

We are called to freedom, Paul proclaims. Many people believe that freedom means doing exactly what they want without regard to its impact on others. In individualistic North America, we hear the following cries of freedom: "It's my money and I can do whatever I want with it," "It's a woman's choice," "It's my property and I will use it as I please," "Don't infringe on my right to gun ownership," "It's not hurting anyone, I can do what I want in my private life." Paul sees Christian freedom from a very different per- spective. Freedom finds its fullest expression in loving relationships that take into consideration the needs of others. Christian freedom is not coercive, it is invitational, and it invites us to let go of our individualistic possessiveness and live in light of God's grace and generosity, manifest in our willingness to sacrifice some aspects of our freedom for the well-being of others and the communities of which we are a part.

"Do not use your freedom as an opportunity for self-indul- gence, but through love become slaves to one another" (5:13). Freedom involves responsibilities as well as rights. In fact, in Chris- tian community, Paul asserts that freedom involves sacrifice for the greater good of those around me. Paul's understanding of freedom within the Christian community is captured in his Letter to the Romans: "I know and am persuaded in the Lord Jesus that noth- ing is unclean in itself; but it is unclean for anyone who thinks it unclean. If your brother or sister is being injured by what you eat, you are no longer walking in love. Do not let what you eat cause the ruin of one for whom Christ died" (Romans 14:14-15). True freedom goes beyond self-interest to embrace the best interests of those with whom we interact.

Living by the Spirit (5:16-26)

Paul's discussion of Christian freedom is elaborated in his contrast of the works of the flesh and the fruit of the Spirit. To avoid misunderstanding, Paul understands the "flesh" as a particu- lar life-orientation rather than a denial of embodiment. Following the Jewish tradition's understanding that the world is inherently good, Paul affirms that the body is the temple of the Holy Spirit (1 Corinthians 6:19). Accordingly, we are called to glorify God in our bodies by treating them with respect and using them in ways that bring well-being to the community. Authentic spirituality truly inspires us to "love him [God] in the world of the flesh," to quote W.H. Auden.

Fleshly living is characterized by self-interest, consumption, greed, and covetousness. Living according to the flesh involves sexually objectifying others and using others for our own gratification. As you ponder Paul's description of the works of the flesh, take an afternoon or evening to view critically the commercials presented on television. What values do they represent? Do they encourage simplicity, care for the earth, healthy relationships, and responsibility to the community? Do commercials promote consumerism, gluttony, intoxication, competition, and superficial sexuality? Fleshly living is all about meeting my needs regardless of my impact on others, the community, or the environment.

In contrast, living in the Spirit involves healthy and life-affirming relationships in which we go beyond self-interest to seek the greatest good for our communities and the world. Living in the Spirit involves going beyond the ego and its needs. Motivated by the mind of Christ (Philippians 2:5-11), we find our joy in breaking down the walls that separate us from our brothers and sisters. We discover our unity with all life and find ourselves at home wherever we go. Authentic spirituality, living in the Spirit, enlarges our souls and enables us to become persons of stature and compassion.

Questions for Discussion

1) Why is "circumcision" such a big deal to Paul? How does it represent slavery and the nullification of grace (5:1-12)? Does the legalism surrounding circumcision really nullify grace?

2) In what ways does God's new creation relativize every human effort? What are the implications of recognizing the limits of our religious practices and beliefs (5:6)?

3) In what ways might love be the "absolute" in Christian experience? How does love fulfill and transcend law and ritual (5:6)?

4) What is your response to Paul's harsh language that his opponents would castrate themselves (5:12)? Why do you think Paul resorts to such harsh language? If you were an editor, would you suggest to Paul that he delete this passage?

5) Yet, grace has its limits. In what ways can freedom go astray? In what ways do we need to use our freedom? What spiritual practices help us to stay on the right path ethically and relationally (5:13-15)?

6) How do the works of the flesh differ from the works of the spirit? What is the primary characteristic of each (5:16-26)?

7) How can we best love God in the world of the flesh? How do we best care for the temple of God in ourselves and others?

Closing Prayer

Holy God, for freedom you have set us free, help us live lovingly and freely, sharing the love we have received to your glory and the well-being of all creation. In Christ's name. Amen.

THE CHURCH OF THE NEW CREATION

GALATIANS 6:1-18

Vision

Participants will reflect on positive relationships within the church and ways we can challenge each other with love. Participants will also reflect on the meaning of new creation and its impact on our understanding of Christian theology, ritual, and spiritual practices. What does it mean to relativize all of our doctrines and practices in light of God's new creation?

Prayer

Begin by a time of thanksgiving for your study and all who were involved in your Bible study. Give thanks for God's presence in the conversations and insights shared. Then, take a moment for silence, quietly opening to divine wisdom.

Spirit of gentleness, move through our lives and inspire us to see Christ in each other. Help us to be faithful to you above all else and place your realm of love above our own personal theologies and rituals. Let love be our goal in all things. In Christ's Name. Amen.

Spirit of Gentleness (6:1-6)

Our unity in Christ is at the heart of Paul's Gospel. In the cross and resurrection, God has created a new community, reflecting God's realm on earth. Being part of God's community challenges

us to treat everyone as God's beloved children, including those with
whom we disagree.

It is ironic that after Paul's passionate denunciation of those
whom he perceives to be perverting the good news of God's grace,
he concludes with a call to gentleness. "If anyone is detected in
a transgression, you who have received the Spirit should restore
such a one in the spirit of gentleness." We don't know if Paul is
referring to a particular behavior in the church or to those who
have succumbed to the message of his opponents and adopted the
Jewish law. But, the message is clear: none of us is perfect and we
will all face the consequences of our actions, and the reality of our
own sinfulness or imperfection should inspire us to reconcile and
care for those who have gone astray. Sin is not always a matter of
willfulness and disobedience. It is often the result of weakness,
addiction, wounds from childhood, low self-esteem, and sins that
have been committed against us. Jesus' parables of grace – the lost
sheep, lost coin, and lost son – reflect three types of waywardness
– simply wandering off, being lost in the shuffle through no fault
of your own, and intentionally following a pathway of self-destruc-
tion. Paul knows firsthand about the inner conflict in which we
desire to the good and end up going against our best resolutions.

All have sinned and fallen short. Still, more importantly, God
loves us and Christ dies for us despite our brokenness and sin.
Grace abounds, when we least expect it and when we think we least
deserve it. Our calling is to let God's grace flow through us to our
imperfect brothers and sisters, enabling them to live by the grace
that has given us new life.

Fair Wages for Spiritual Leaders

Throughout Galatians, there is a subtle undercurrent that
connects our theological perspectives with issues of justice and
equality. Belief inspires behavior both in terms of interpersonal
and community relationships. This may even shape our economic
decision-making. Accordingly, there is also a grace in pastoral com-

pensation. In a passage that appears out of context, Paul counsels that "those who are taught the word must share in all good things with their teacher" (5:6). Just as we desire fair compensation for ourselves, we should insure that our spiritual leaders are also fairly compensated so that they can focus on their calling as apostles of grace. Perhaps, this passage should lead to a conversation about staff salaries, not only as they relate to the ministerial staff, but also the sexton or janitor, office administrator, and any part-time employees.

Sowing and Reaping (5:7-10)

Paul is realistic about the consequences of sin even after we have experienced God's unmerited and unconditional grace. We all have history and must come to terms with it in spite of the new life we experience in Christ. In twelve step groups, participants discover that it is essential that we make amends and ask forgiveness from those whom we have hurt as a result of our enslavement to alcohol and other addictive behaviors. Love is not "never having to say you're sorry," as the film *Love Story* suggested. Love and grace involve the constant willingness to forgive and ask for forgiveness for sins of commission and omission.

All have fallen short of God's vision. Good people, who have experienced God's grace, may no longer be committing obvious sins. Our sinfulness is much more subtle and even socially-acceptable. The harm we inflict on others is often unnoticed yet still hurtful: lack of attention to others' needs, busyness with important and good projects that keeps us away from home, inattentiveness to others' feelings, failure to confront injustice, or receiving indirect benefits from unjust social and economic structures. We constantly need to make a spiritual and relational inventory, asking ourselves, "Are we treating our loved ones, brothers and sisters, and fellow creatures as God's beloved children?" Many a minister has been spiritually "convicted" when her or his spouse or child says the following: "I wish you thought our relationship was as important as spending four nights this week and half of Saturday at church meetings." "You spend more time with the youth group than you do with me."

Ethics is profoundly theocentric. Our love of God is reflected in our love for the world beloved by God. Ethics involves making our lives and actions a gift to God. For as we have done unto the least of these, we have done unto God (Matthew 25:34-40).

Graceful action flows from God's grace to us. As Martin Luther says, we are "little Christs," who bring wholeness and love to others from the love we have received. In our daily lives, Paul counsels to "not grow weary of doing what is right.... whenever we have an opportunity, let us work for the good of all, and especially for those in the family of faith" (6:9-10). Seize the moment! Let your life be a living witness to the grace you have received.

A New Creation Is Everything (6:11-18)

Paul dismisses his "administrative assistant" and concludes Galatians with his own pen to give emphasis to the key points of his message. He reiterates the need for them to stay on course and not submit to slavery to the well-intended but wrong perspectives of his opponents. He reaffirms that centrality of the cross and the importance of a sacrificial, spirit-centered cross-shaped life. He then reaches a spiritual crescendo with another classic theological passage: "For neither circumcision or uncircumcision is anything, but a new creation is everything" (6:15). Our theological positions and rituals matter, but all of them are imperfect and relative in relationship to the one key thing: God's new creation meditated through the grace of Jesus Christ. As Paul was to say elsewhere, "but we have this treasure in clay jars, so that it may be made clear that this extraordinary power belongs to God and does not come from us" (2 Corinthians 4:7).

The Zen Buddhists say, "don't confuse the finger pointing at the moon with the moon itself." This is good advice, especially for ardent believers. Don't make idols of your theological beliefs, liturgical practices, doctrinal statements, or congregational traditions or rituals. God is always doing a new thing and bringing forth a new creation. Faithfulness embraces our past – whether the Jewish law or the traditions of our denomination or congregation. Faithfulness also opens us up to a grace that challenges us to hospitality to the stranger, creativity in responding to the diverse cultures and lifestyles of time, and openness to sharing the message in ways that include seekers, spiritual but not religious persons, and former churchgoers who have been traumatized by the behavior of their fellow Christians.

Paul concludes with a fairly common benediction. But there is nothing common in Paul's blessing, given Paul's passionate message to communities trying to discern Christ's way in their lives. "May the grace of our Lord Jesus Christ be with your spirit, brothers and sisters. Amen." Thanks be to God for the freedom we have in Jesus Christ, our companion, friend, and healer.

Questions for Discussion

1) What does it mean to bear one another's burdens (6:1-2)?
2) How does Paul approach bad behavior among church folk? How should we respond when people cause a fuss in the community (6:1-2)?
3) "If anyone is detected in a transgression, you who have received the Spirit should restore such a one in the spirit of gentleness." What might Peter's response have been if he had the opportunity to read these words? Would he have reminded Paul how he criticized him publically?
4) Paul asserts that "those who are taught the word must share in all good things with their teacher" (6:6). What implications might this have for clergy compensation?
5) What do you think we reap when we sow in the spirit? And, conversely, in the flesh (6:7-10)?

6) Why do you think Paul concludes the letter with a note that he personally inscribes? Why do you think he makes a point of speaking of writing in large letters (6:11)?

7) What does it mean to boast of the cross of Christ Jesus? What does it mean to crucify the world (6:14)?

8) What does the phrase "new creation" mean to you? In what ways does the new creation relativize every other spiritual or ethical achievement or doctrinal position (6:15)?

Closing Prayer

Loving God, as we conclude this study, may your word continue to inspire us, guiding us to be persons of love and hospitality, welcoming strangers, and sharing the grace we have received, until all persons see themselves as your beloved children. In Jesus' name. Amen.

APPENDIX A

BOOKS FOR THE
ADVENTUROUS READER

Bassler, Joette. *Navigating Paul: An Introduction to Key Theological Concepts*. (Louisville: Westminster/John Knox) 1997.

Borg, Marcus and John Dominic Crossan. *The First Paul: Reclaiming the Radical Visionary Behind the Church's Conservative Icon*. (New York: Harper One) 2009.

Carey, Greg. *Sinners: Jesus and His Earliest Followers*. (Waco: Baylor University Press) 2009.

Dunn, James D.G. *The Epistle to the Galatians*. (Grand Rapids: Baker Academic Books) 1993.

Dunn, James D.G. *The Theology of Paul's Letter to the Galatians*. (Cambridge: Cambridge University Press) 1993.

Epperly, Bruce. *Healing Marks: Healing and Spirituality in Mark's Gospel*. (Gonzalez; FL: Energion Publications) 2012.

_____. *Holistic Spirituality: Life-giving Wisdom from the Letter of James*. (Gonzalez, FL: Energion Publications) 2014.

_____. *Philippians: A Participatory Study Guide*. (Gonzalez, FL: Energion Publications) 2011.

_____. *Transforming Acts: Acts of the Apostles as a 21st Century Gospel*. (Gonzalez, FL, Energion Publications) 2013.

Hays, Richard. *The Letter to the Galatians: Introduction, Commentary, and Reflections*. (The New Interpreter's Bible, Volume XI. Nashville: Abingdon Press) 2000.

Lull, David. *The Spirit in Galatia: Paul's Interpretation of Pneuma as Divine Power*. (Eugene, OR: Wipf and Stock Publishers) 1980.

Wright, N.T. *Paul and the Faithfulness of God*. Two Volumes. (Minneapolis: Fortress Press) 2013.

TOOLS FOR LIFE-TRANSFORMING BIBLE STUDY

Scripture is a living word, embracing body, mind, spirit, and relationships. Although our primary resource for understanding scripture is our openness to becoming transformed by the Holy Spirit as a result of our prayerful commitment to spiritual practices along with our willingness to accept God's radical and unconditional grace for us and others, we can also love God with our minds by consulting intellectually-solid versions of scripture along with sound and faithful commentaries. The following are some suggested resources to deepen your encounter with Galatians and any other biblical text[14]:

BIBLE VERSIONS

There are many excellent versions of scripture beyond the ones I recommend. You can get a feel for the varieties of biblical translations by consulting Bible Gateway on-line. Put out by Zondervan, it contains over one hundred translations and paraphrases, that are easily accessible.

(See www.BibleGateway.com)

Here are some translations and paraphrases I regularly consult:

Accessible to virtually every adult reader
— *Contemporary English Version* (CEV)
Written 3rd or 4th grade reading level; high degree of accuracy within the context of its aim for easy readability.

---

14 Much of this section is based on Bruce Epperly, *Philippians: A Participatory Study Guide*. (Gonzalez, FL: Energion Publications, 2011.)

— *The Cotton Patch Version* by Clarence Jordan

An interpretive paraphrase reflecting rural Georgia dialect and culture. It reminds us that God comes to us in terms of our concrete experience and not some abstract, timeless world. Simply fun to read.

— *The Message* by Eugene Peterson

Heavily paraphrased with cultural terms translated. This version is fun to read, and enables us to experience God's voice in the voices of North American Christians. However, it tends to obscure elements of the original cultures.

— *New Living Translation* (NLT)

A more accurate revision of the Living Bible. This is the easy-reading Bible intended intially for evangelical Christians.

— *Today's New International Version*

Shows its relationship to the popular NIV in many wordings, but uses simplified language and sentence structure in many cases.

For study or reading

— *Common English Bible* (CEB)

A new translation sponsored by mainline or moderate Protestant publishing houses, the CEB attempts to combine high level scholarship with readability.

— *New International Version* (NIV)

The NIV is a dynamic equivalent translation of the Bible that is popular among evangelical Christians.

— *New Revised Standard Version* (NRSV)

The descendant of the Revised Standard Version, it is the Bible of choice for mainline or moderate/progressive Christians needing a study Bible. It is known for its attempt to use gender neutral language where appropriate.

— *Revised English Bible* (REB)

This version was translated by an interdenominational/ecumenical committee with interfaith review that exhibits the different texture of British English.

— New American Standard Bible (NASB)

A very formal rendering of the original languages, the NASB has its roots in conservative evangelicalism.

STUDY BIBLES

Study Bibles usually contain introductory articles giving the Biblical context, information on methodology and overviews of various themes in the Bible. They will also include introductions to each book and comments on difficult passages. Study Bibles will reflect religious views of editors and authors, some more than others. Care should be taken to distinguish the Biblical text from the comments, and facts and opinions within the comments.

– New Interpreter's Study Bible (NRSV)

This new study Bible includes extensive historical and theological annotations, good introductions and outlines, and excursuses giving further background and insight regarding particular themes and passages.

– New Oxford Annotated Bible (NRSV)

A standard scholarly study Bible, often used in universities and seminaries.

– Harper Collins Study Bible (NRSV)

Carrying the sponsorship of the Society of Biblical Literature, it has mainstream or liberal notes with acknowledgment of more conservative options.

– The NIV Study Bible (Zondervan)

Popular among evangelicals, bringing a more conservative approach to Biblical interpretation and study.

BIBLE HANDBOOKS

Bible handbooks provide historical and cultural information, usually with a number of general articles and then comments on particular books and passages. Using a Bible handbook along with your Bible is like having a Bible with study notes, though usually having a handbook in a separate volume will mean that the handbook contains more exhaustive information. Bible handbooks, like study Bibles, will reflect religious presuppositions of the editors.

Mainstream and/or Liberal
– *The Cambridge Companion to the Bible*
– *Oxford Companion to the Bible*
Moderate
Eerdman's Handbook to the Bible
Conservative
– *Zondervan's Handbook to the Bible*

BIBLE COMMENTARIES

Bible commentaries are designed to provide introductions, background, and interpretation of biblical texts. They come in many forms, ranging from one-volume efforts to commentaries on individual books. Many commentaries appear in sets, but with few exceptions, when purchasing commentaries on individual books of the Bible it is better to buy these individually rather than in sets.

Mainstream
— *New Interpreter's Bible*, 12 volumes (Abingdon)
A replacement for the venerable *Interpreter's Bible*, this is a mainstream commentary set drawing its authors from across the Christian community, including evangelical, mainline, Catholic, and Orthodox scholars.

— *New Interpeter's One Volume Commentary* (Abingdon)

Based on the principles of the much larger multi-volume edition, it is a completely new commentary and not simply an abridgement.

— *HarperCollins Bible Commentary* (HarperOne)

As with the HarperCollins Bible Dictionary, this commentary is sponsored by the Society of Biblical Literature.

— *People's New Testament Commentary of the New Testament* (WJK Press)

This commentary on the New Testament is written by two Disciples of Christ scholars, Fred Craddock and Eugene Boring.

— *The New Jerome Bible Commentary, 3rd edition* (Prentice Hall)

This is a predominantly Roman Catholic commentary, authored and edited by highly regarded critical scholars.

Evangelical

— *Eerdmans Commentary on the Bible*

This work is very compatible with mainstream scholarship, but comes from a publisher that stands as a bridge between evangelical and mainline Protestantism.

— *New Bible Commentary: 21st Century edition* (IVP)

BIBLE CONCORDANCES

Concordances may be exhaustive, complete, or concise. Usage of these terms is not 100% consistent. In addition they may either be either organized by words or topics. Many Bibles contain small, concise concordances. Many study Bibles contain topical concordances. Exhaustive concordances contain every reference to a word listed under every word. Complete concordances contain references to each and every verse, using significant terms, though not necessarily under every word in the verse. Concise concordances contain selective references and may not reference all verses. Topical concordances provide a guide to topics covered by specific texts. This can be helpful, but one must always remember that unlike a typical concordance, which is rooted inword usage, this type is more likely to be driven by theological presuppositions. Concordances with Greek and/or Hebrew Lexicons (dictionaries or vocabularies) can be useful, but one should remember that translation is not as simple as just picking a word from a dictionary definition. Context always determines usage and meaning.

Exhaustive with Greek/Hebrew
— *Strong's Exhaustive Concordance*

It is part of the public domain and is regularly reprinted. It is based on the King James Version and an older lexicon. It's numbering system and lexicon has served as the model for other concordances.

— *The NIV Exhaustive Concordance* (Zondervan)

Based completely on the NIV, it goes beyond Strong's.

— *New American Standard Exhaustive Concordance of the Bible/Hebrew-Aramaic and Greek Dictionaries*

— *New American Standard Strong's Exhaustive Concordance*

Based on the Strong's Concordance system, it is keyed to the NASB.

Exhaustive Concordances
— *NRSV Concordance Unabridged* (Zondervan)

Keyed to the NSRV.

Concise Concordances
— *The Concise Concordance to the New Revised Standard Version* (Oxford)

Topical Concordances
— *Holman Concise Topical Concordance* (Holman Reference)

— *Topical Analysis of the Bible* (Baker)

BIBLE DICTIONARIES

Bible dictionaries provide definitions of various biblical terms, information about places and people, and introductory information about biblical books. Most information contained in a Bible handbook can be found in a Bible dictionary, but it will be organized much differently.

The religious views of authors and editors will impact the content of a Bible dictionary, as it does with a handbook or commentary. When purchasing a Bible dictionary, it is always best to purchase one that has been authored/edited by reputable scholars, is even-handed in its approach, and is up-to-date.

Mainstream

— *HarperCollins Bible Dictionary, Revised Edition*. (HarperOne)

— *A Dictionary of the Bible, 2nd edition*. (Oxford UniversityPress)

Based upon the Harper-Collins Bible Dictionary, this is a more up-to-date expansion.

— *Anchor Bible Dictionary*, 6 volumes (Doubleday)

— *Eerdman's Dictionary of the Bible*

— *New Interpreter's Dictionary of the Bible*, 5 volumes (Abingdon)

Evangelical

— *New International Bible Dictionary* (Zondervan)

— *New Bible Dictionary, 3rd edition*. (Intervarsity Press)

— *Zondervan Encyclopedia of the Bible, Revised Edition*, 5 volumes

BIBLE ATLASES

Bible atlases contain maps and related background materials that assist students of the bible placing texts and individuals in their proper historical and geographical context.

It is important once again to stress the need for up-to-date reference works. It is also important to note that theology once again impacts the results of the work. Knowing the background of a publisher can be helpful in this. Therefore, HarperCollins is probably more mainstream and cross-confessional, while IVP and Zondervan will be more evangelical or conservative.

HarperCollins Concise Atlas of the Bible. (HarperOne)
In paperback, this one may be all the average Bible student needs.
The MacMillan Bible Atlas, 3rd edition. (MacMillan)
This has been a standard atlas, which is marked by the editorship of Jewish scholars.
The Biblical World (National Geographic)
HarperCollins Atlas of Bible History (HarperOne)
Oxford Bible Atlas (Oxford University Press)
The IVP Atlas of Bible History. (IVP)
Zondervan Atlas of the Bible (Zondervan)

SOME DEFINITIONS

Note: Labels in connection with many of these resources can be misleading. No label is to be regarded as either pejorative or complimentary. "Mainstream" doesn't mean "correct," for example.

Mainstream: Materials which would be suitable for use in departments of religion at secular universities, most seminaries, and moderate and progressive Christian congregations. This does not imply more or less correct in content

Interfaith: Involving persons other than those of one faith (Christians and Jews, for example). Distinguish from interdenominational, or ecumenical.

Evangelical: A high view of biblical authority, with particular emphasis on divine sovereignty and the Lordship of Christ.

ALSO IN THE PARTICIPATORY STUDY SERIES

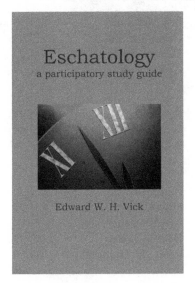

Eschatology
a participatory study guide

Edward W. H. Vick

... a helpful corrective and foundation for a subject that has become untethered from the Bible, theology, and reality.

Rev. Dr. Geoffrey D. Lentz
First United Methodist Church
Pensacola, Florida

... a solid presentation of the historical, sociological, and ideological issues that arise from reading Phillippians.

Lisa Davison
Professor of Hebrew Bible
Phillips Theological Seminary

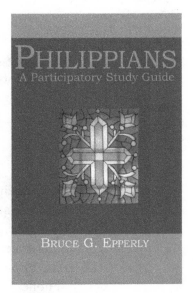

PHILIPPIANS
A Participatory Study Guide

BRUCE G. EPPERLY

MORE FROM ENERGION PUBLICATIONS

Personal Study

Holy Smoke! Unholy Fire!	Bob McKibben	$14.99
The Jesus Paradigm	David Alan Black	$17.99
When People Speak for God	Henry Neufeld	$17.99
The Sacred Journey	Chris Surber	$11.99

Christian Living

Faith in the Public Square	Robert D. Cornwall	$16.99
Grief: Finding the Candle of Light	Jody Neufeld	$8.99
Crossing the Street	Robert LaRochelle	$16.99

Bible Study

Learning and Living Scripture	Lentz/Neufeld	$12.99
From Inspiration to Understanding	Edward W. H. Vick	$24.99
Luke: A Participatory Study Guide	Geoffrey Lentz	$8.99
Philippians: A Participatory Study Guide	Bruce Epperly	$9.99
Ephesians: A Participatory Study Guide	Robert D. Cornwall	$9.99

Theology

Creation in Scripture	Herold Weiss	$12.99
Creation: the Christian Doctrine	Edward W. H. Vick	$12.99
The Politics of Witness	Allan R. Bevere	$9.99
Ultimate Allegiance	Robert D. Cornwall	$9.99
History and Christian Faith	Edward W. H. Vick	$9.99
The Church Under the Cross	William Powell Tuck	$11.99
The Journey to the Undiscovered Country	William Powell Tuck	$9.99
Eschatology: A Participatory Study Guide	Edward W. H. Vick	$9.99

Ministry

Clergy Table Talk	Kent Ira Groff	$9.99
Out of This World	Darren McClellan	$24.99
Wind and Whirlwind	David Moffett-Moore	$9.99

Generous Quantity Discounts Available
Dealer Inquiries Welcome
Energion Publications — P.O. Box 841
Gonzalez, FL_ 32560
Website: http://energionpubs.com
Phone: (850) 525-3916